- Someone in my family has been diagnosed with depression. I know I'm probably at higher risk for getting depressed, but how high is my risk?

- What factors increase the risk of inheriting depression?

- Is there a link between alcoholism and chronic depression?

- Everything seems to be going all right in my life, but I still feel depressed. Why?

- Is there a cure for depression?

You'll find the answers to these and many other questions in this important and life-enhancing book.

IF IT RUNS IN YOUR FAMILY

DEPRESSION

REDUCING YOUR RISK

Connie S. Chan, Ph.D.

Foreword by Barbara DeBetz, M.D.

Developed by The Philip Lief Group, Inc.

BANTAM BOOKS
NEW YORK · TORONTO · LONDON · SYDNEY · AUCKLAND

This book is not intended as a substitute for the medical advice of physicians. The reader should regularly consult a physician in matters relating to his or her health and particularly with respect to any symptoms that may require diagnosis or medical attention. Readers should also speak with their own doctors about their own individual needs before starting any diet or fitness program. Consulting one's personal physician about diet and exercise is especially important if the reader is on any medication or is already under medical care for any illness.

IF IT RUNS IN YOUR FAMILY: DEPRESSION

A Bantam Book / November 1993

ISBN 0-553-56382-3

Published simultaneously in the United States and Canada

Bantam Books are published by Bantam Books, a division of Bantam Doubleday Dell Publishing Group, Inc. Its trademark, consisting of the words "Bantam Books" and the portrayal of a rooster, is Registered in U.S. Patent and Trademark Office and in other countries. Marca Registrada. Bantam Books, 1540 Broadway, New York, New York 10036.

For my parents,
John and Lorraine,
and my brother, Tony.

Acknowledgments

I would like to thank my editors at The Philip Lief Group: Nancy Kalish, Robyn Feller, Patty O'Connell, Cathy Hemming, Julia Banks, and the late Jamie Rothstein for their expert assistance and encouragement in the preparation of this book. I am also thankful to my friends for their unwavering support and help that allowed me to complete this book.

C.S.C.

Acknowledgments

Contents

Foreword

Humankind has always known mood disorders, and millions of people and their families have suffered from depression in its varying forms and intensities. Over the past twenty years, however, we have seen major advances in the diagnosis and treatment of depression. Depressed individuals no longer have to struggle through incapacitating and lengthy episodes of this illness. With proper treatment, depression may be prevented, or at least its severity diminished, and the overall quality of life of those afflicted with this disease can be drastically improved.

This book gives the latest information about the nature and course of depression. It also describes different treatment methods that are currently used. Dr. Connie Chan gives the reader the large body of current knowledge in a clear and practical way without oversimplifying the psychological and social issues involved.

Depression is one of the most common psychiatric

disorders. It is a disturbance of affect—in other words, a mood disorder. Although everybody has, at one time or another, felt "blue," "down," or in "the dumps," as much as 20 percent of the general population go one step further and proceed to develop a clinical depression. For anyone who shows the signs and symptoms of depression, especially if accompanied by suicidal tendencies, the signals must be taken seriously.

Over the last two decades there has been a wide range of new findings in the area of affective disorders; the pendulum has swung from viewing depression as a purely mental disturbance to our present understanding that it is both psychological and biological. Lengthy psychotherapy and/or heroic methods (undertaken only if necessary to save life) such as ECT (electroconvulsive therapies) have given way to treatment using cognitive behavioral approaches, antidepressant medications, and various other forms of psychotherapy in combination with medication. Results are achieved more quickly and often more dramatically.

The term *depression* is a general one and most people use it loosely. However, in order to treat and prevent depression effectively in those who have a predisposition to it, it has to be diagnosed accurately. Most clinicians use the criteria described in the *Diagnostic and Statistical Manual of Mental Disorders* (DSM) of the American Psychiatric Association, which classifies depressive disorders as (1) major depression, single episode or recurrent, (2) depressive neurosis (called dysthemia), and (3) depressive disorders that show signs and symptoms of depression but do not meet the criteria of the other two. In this last group you find depression superimposed over another mental illness such as schizophrenia, or in combination with a state of anxiety; and stress-related depressive episodes, or depression in association with a major change in life events, such as physical illness, death of a family member, or a divorce.

These disorders involve periodic disturbances in mood, appetite, energy level, activity level, concentration, and various other aspects of behavior. The individual's social relations, as well as every day functioning, are usually affected, having a serious impact on the entire family. In the worst scenario, feelings of helplessness, hopelessness, and low self-esteem can lead the depressed individual to contemplate and even act upon suicidal impulses.

Psychiatric research is trying to explore the genetic transmission of depression. Empirically, we always knew that depression "runs in families," but now, with new techniques, genetic research has come closer to identifying a gene marker that would enable clinicians to test high-risk individuals—those who have inherited the gene that causes depression. Remarkably, this will allow us to identify those who would be most likely to suffer from this illness, and to take effective preventive measures. Being informed about the signs and symptoms of depression and knowing the risk factors are the first steps toward prevention in families who have a history of depression. Effective help *is* available. Most clinicians and therapists are aware of the different treatment methods and medications available and are able to develop a treatment strategy that works. Although depression is a serious illness, there's good news—it's treatable. With the proper diagnosis and prompt treatment, complete recovery occurs in most cases.

This book erases some of the misconceptions about depression, bringing a fresh, new understanding to those afflicted with this disease as well as to their families.

BARBARA DEBETZ, M.D.
Practicing psychiatrist

1

What It Means to Be at Risk

A successful professional secretary in her early thirties, Susan* seemed to have it all: a loving husband, comfortable home, and good looks. But things had started to go wrong. Susan had begun to feel that her life was slowly slipping away from her in ways she could no longer control. Nothing was fun any more; everything had become an unpleasant chore. Susan went to work as usual, but found she couldn't concentrate and often ended up wasting the day, sleeping in her chair with the door closed. When she returned home nothing in the refrigerator seemed appealing. She would hope that her husband had to work late so she wouldn't have to talk to him. If he did come home, she told him she was ill and went to bed. But she couldn't fall asleep. Instead, Susan would lie in bed and worry about all the work

*All names and identifying information of individuals mentioned in this book have been changed to protect their privacy.

1

she had left undone at the office, all the bills unpaid at home, all the telephone calls from family and friends unreturned. She was so ashamed of feeling so utterly hopeless and helpless that she dared not tell anyone.

Lying in bed, crying into her pillow, Susan remembered the happy, carefree days of her childhood. But she also remembered her mother wearing her pajamas all day, staying in her room, quietly sobbing behind the closed door. As a child, Susan hadn't understood what was wrong with her mother. She recalled that usually after a week or two her mother seemed to feel better and became lively again, resuming her duties and taking care of the family. Long periods of time would pass until her mother withdrew again, usually for several weeks, only to return once more.

One night, Susan realized what her mother had been experiencing during those periods of staying in her room. "She must have felt like I do now," she thought, "overwhelmed, helpless, and hopeless. Like a failure, worthless. No wonder my mother stayed in her room all day. Who can bear to face anyone when you feel so despairing?"

Susan had repressed the painful memories of her mother's episodes of depression for years, but now, in her thirties, she was beginning to succumb to the same overwhelming feelings of sadness, hopelessness, and despair. The thought of being like her mother, suffering recurring bouts of depression throughout her life, terrified her. "Does depression run in my family?" she thought. "How can I cope with this? Is there a way to break this pattern?"

Susan is, indeed, at a higher risk for depression because of her family history. But although she feels very isolated, she is by no means alone.

Depression affects millions of people. It is so pervasive that it is considered to be the "common cold" of mental illness. It is the oldest known psychiatric disorder, first written about by the ancient Greeks. At any given time, about 6 percent of the population suffers from serious depression. An estimated 30 million to 40 million Americans will experience depressive illness at least once in their lifetimes, and 30 to 40 percent of those will struggle through recurring bouts of depression.

Depression is also a serious, life-threatening illness. Many victims are driven to suicide, accounting for over 60 percent of all suicides. All in all, 15 percent of the individuals who suffer from affective (mood) disorders (the overwhelming majority from depressive mood disorder) commit suicide. In spite of the seriousness of this illness, however, it is estimated that 80 percent of those who suffer from depression do not receive treatment. That's because symptoms of depression are often masked by physical illness, alcoholism, or drug addiction, or go unrecognized. In addition, people in our society often feel guilty or fear stigmatization for having a mental illness and will not acknowledge the problem. While depression can be treated quite successfully, the longer it is untreated, the more likely it is to become recurrent, chronic, and severely debilitating.

Who Is at Risk?

Despite recent advances in the treatment of this disorder, more and more people are becoming depressed. In fact, the rate of diagnosed depression in the United

States, and around the world, has increased greatly among individuals born after World War II. Consider these facts:

- Fifty years ago depression was considered an illness that affected those between forty and sixty years old. The average age of onset of depression has declined, however, to the mid-twenties, according to the National Institute of Mental Health (NIMH).
- For men, the likelihood of experiencing a major depression is 1 in 10. For women, it is 1 in 4, more than twice as much.
- Adults are not the only people affected by depression—it is also estimated that 6 to 7 percent of adolescents could be diagnosed as having depressive illness.
- In addition, perhaps as many as 2 percent of children between six and twelve years old suffer from depression.

What Causes Depression?

The good news is that significant progress has been made in the understanding and treatment of depressive illness over the last decade. Once commonly thought to be purely a state of mind or caused by character defects, it is now viewed as an illness, like diabetes or high blood pressure. Depressive illness develops as a result of an interplay between biological and psychological factors. Scientists believe that individuals who suffer from depression have a *predisposition* to this illness. In other words, it is likely that they are born with a genetic susceptibility to depression.

A number of factors, including environmental ones, such as stressful events, or changes in the body's chemistry, may trigger the symptoms of depressive illness. Yet even with a predisposition, some individuals will never suffer from depression. That's because many different elements play a role in determining whether a person who is at risk will be affected.

What Can You Do?

This book will help you to decide if you, like Susan, are at risk for depression, and if so, will teach you how to take *preventive* measures to reduce the likelihood of your suffering from depressive illness. Step by step, you will learn about depression, how to determine your risk factors, and how this illness can be presented and treated. Your understanding of depression, self-diagnosis, and attitudes can mean the difference between suffering from recurrent bouts of misery and living a fulfilling, symptom-free life. The key is in your hands, in the information you are about to receive. Being at risk does not mean you are doomed to despair and depression. Prevention and treatment of the symptoms of this disease are very possible if you are aware of the problem and start *now*.

What Is Depression, Anyway?

Depression comes in different forms and affects people in different ways. The types that receive the most attention from the medical establishment are:

Major unipolar depression—debilitating depression

that leaves a person feeling lethargic, dull, and filled with an overwhelming and continuous sense of despair for eighteen months, on the average. (This book deals primarily with unipolar depression.)

Major endogenous depression—not apparently triggered by any life event, with what clinicians call "vegetative" symptoms such as insomnia, lethargy, psychomotor retardation (a general slowing of mental and physical activity), and an extremely hopeless, depressed mood. This occurs most frequently in those with a family history of depression. Since it responds better to drug treatment than to psychotherapy, its cause is thought to be biochemical. The risk of inheriting this type of depression if it runs in your family is higher than the risk for more moderate forms.

Bipolar disorder—more commonly known as *manic-depression*, during which an individual alternates between manic states of frenzied activity accompanied by a sense of being able to do everything and anything, and depressive states in which he or she "crashes" into the depths of despair, becoming immobilized and debilitated.

Chronic mild depression, a previously ignored moderate form of the illness that is separate from other types of depression, is estimated to affect large numbers of people. These people may not exhibit severe symptoms of depression, but they suffer a chronic low-level depression. These individuals function daily by going to work and can usually maintain relationships, but they feel as though they are constantly under a heavy burden. They have low levels of energy and experience the world as a gloomy, discouraging place.

Depression also takes on many other forms within this range. This illness is best understood by realizing that depression occurs on a continuum, with the ordinary feelings of being down in the dumps or sad on one end and the major debilitating, serious, and even life-threatening kinds of depression that require hospitalization on the other.

Michael, thirty-one, is an example of a chronic mild depressive. He works as a lawyer in a small law firm. "It is an effort to do everything, including going to work," he explains.

Since I feel down much of the time, I avoid answering the phone at home or going out. I used to watch TV, but the programs are either depressing (like the news or dramas) or so relentlessly cheerful that I can't relate to them. I feel like I'm living under a black cloud that follows me wherever I go. Things are just so discouraging in my life that I have little energy to pursue anything beyond my daily duties of going to work and returning home.

Now and then, all of us feel down or discouraged. We might be turned down for a job, or rejected for a date, and feel keenly disappointed, even depressed for a day or two. Maybe even three or four days. But there is a big difference between a short bout of depression and something far more serious. Yet, many people cannot tell the difference between transitory, minor depression and the more serious depressive illness. In fact, some people don't even recognize the symptoms of depression, and thus, don't seek any help.

This book will help you understand the different

manifestations of depression. It will address the more serious kinds of depression—the kind that won't go away, as well as the mild forms that keep returning over and over again. There are ways in which you can be helped if your depressive symptoms seem to linger or return after a symptom-free period.

What Are the Symptoms of Depression?

How do you know if you or someone you know is depressed, and to what extent? The following Depression Self-Test will help you to determine if you are depressed. Answer the questions honestly, circling the response that best describes the way you feel.

Depression Self-Test

1. I feel sad and unhappy.   a. always   b. sometimes   c. rarely

2. I have trouble concentrating. Sometimes I cannot complete simple tasks.   a. always   b. sometimes   c. rarely

3. Very few things hold my interest. Most activities are more trouble than they are worth.   a. always   b. sometimes   c. rarely

4. I have trouble   a. always   b. sometimes   c. rarely
   making
   decisions.

5. I have sleep   a. always   b. sometimes   c. rarely
   problems:
   trouble falling
   asleep, waking
   up too early,
   or great diffi-
   culty waking
   up in the
   morning.

6. I feel restless   a. always   b. sometimes   c. rarely
   and irritable.
   Nothing
   seems to
   please me.

7. I feel tired   a. always   b. sometimes   c. rarely
   and drained.

8. My appetite   a. always   b. sometimes   c. rarely
   has changed.
   I am either
   overeating or
   undereating.

9. I feel like   a. always   b. sometimes   c. rarely
   crying much
   of the time.

10. I feel little   a. always   b. sometimes   c. rarely
    hope about
    the future.

11. I feel so dis-   a. always   b. sometimes   c. rarely
    couraged that
    I feel like end-
    ing my life.
12. I have little   a. always   b. sometimes   c. rarely
    interest in sex.
13. Other people   a. always   b. sometimes   c. rarely
    are more suc-
    cessful than
    me. I feel like
    a failure most
    of the time.
14. I feel guilty   a. always   b. sometimes   c. rarely
    about many
    things.
15. There is little   a. always   b. sometimes   c. rarely
    that I enjoy.

Score by assigning 2 points to *a*, 1 point to *b*, 0 points
to *c*.

SCORING: 0–9 Normal feelings of being down on
         occasion.
         10–15 Mild depression—You feel down
         more often than is considered normal. De-
         pression *sometimes* interferes with your en-
         joyment of life.
         16–25 Moderate chronic depression—You
         face a constant battle against despairing, sad,
         and unhappy feelings.
         26–30 Severe depression—Depression is se-
         riously affecting and debilitating your life.

Any score above 15 indicates that you should consider
professional treatment to help you to get rid of these

symptoms of depression which are depleting the quality of your life.

The common symptoms of depression include:

- Feelings of helplessness—You feel powerless and that you have lost control of your life. "I can't change anything, so why bother?" you say.
- Feelings of sadness—You cry frequently, feel a sense of hopelessness, loneliness, and unhappiness.
- Loss of interest—You no longer find pleasure in activities you used to enjoy. You have little interest in having sex.
- Low self-esteem or guilt—You feel like you can't do anything right, are disappointed in yourself, feel guilty for letting other people down.
- Sleep disturbances—You have trouble falling asleep, or you wake up in the middle of the night and can't go back to sleep, or you wake up early in the morning. You may also sleep too much or have great difficulty waking up in the morning.
- Restlessness and irritability—You feel dissatisfied, irritable all the time. You are extra sensitive to other people's criticisms or comments.
- Thoughts of suicide and death—You feel like giving it all up sometimes. "Why bother living?" you ask. "I am so miserable that I have nothing to live for."
- Difficulty concentrating—You have trouble focusing on your work, and simple tasks seem very difficult.
- Eating Disturbances—Your lack of appetite and interest in eating has resulted in weight loss, or your overeating and binging on food has resulted in weight gain.

- Chronic pains that do not respond to appropriate treatment—You suffer persisting physical symptoms such as headaches or chest pains, and have an increased susceptibility to physical illness such as colds, flu.
- Pessimism and gloominess—You don't expect things to work out for you because they never do.
- Increased alcohol or drug usage—You use these drugs as a means of escape from feelings of depression.

A person who is depressed is unlikely to experience *all* of these symptoms but will probably experience many of them. The way to tell more severe depression from its milder forms is by the intensity and duration of the symptoms. Obviously, the more intense the symptoms are, and the longer they persist, the more serious the depression. If the symptoms are present on a daily basis for longer than two weeks, then an individual can be considered to be suffering from moderate to serious clinical depression. Even if symptoms do not last for as long as two weeks but come and go sporadically, they can result in great suffering and misery. With proper awareness and appropriate treatment, you can deal with your symptoms of depression and free yourself from the feelings of unhappiness and hopelessness.

The Genetic Component

More and more, scientists have found evidence to demonstrate that depression, from mild to severe, runs in families. Often, depression can be traced back through many generations. Much like the genetic traits for other illnesses, such as high blood pressure, diabetes, and alcoholism, which can be passed on from one generation to the next, the genetic predisposition for depression can be inherited from one or both of your parents or your grandparents. It is still unclear as to whether there is one gene or several genes that carry the susceptibility to depression, but those who inherit this genetic predisposition to depressive illness are at risk and are much more vulnerable.

For example, Susan's family has passed on the genetic predisposition to depression. She is the youngest of three children, with an older brother and sister. While Susan has only recently begun to suffer from mild symptoms, her older brother, Matt, has survived two suicide attempts.

When Matt was twenty-four, he suffered a nervous breakdown, became severely despondent and depressed, and made an unsuccessful suicide attempt. Following a six-month hospitalization, he seemed to recover completely. He showed few symptoms of depression for four years, but then became inexplicably unhappy again. Matt withdrew into his home and lay in bed for days, until he tried again to kill himself with an overdose of drugs. This time his hospitalization lasted three months. In the six years since then, with the help of medication and therapy, he has been managing his depression well.

Susan had always known that her brother suffered from depression, but never thought it had anything to do with her own vulnerability to depressive illness. Besides, he had always been a little more prone to moodiness as a child, and neither Susan nor her sister suffered from moodiness other than the usual unhappiness now and then. As far as Susan knows, her sister, who is an energetic, active teacher, does not have any symptoms of depression.

When asked about her parents, Susan, as mentioned earlier in this chapter, recalled that her mother did have a few episodes in which she stayed in her room for weeks at a time. At the time, Susan never quite understood what her mother had been ill with during those periods, but she assumed it was a physical illness that made her tired, something like mononucleosis. It was only recently, in the course of being interviewed for this book, that Susan could recall that her mother did seem very sad and sometimes cried in bed during her illness. It seems so long ago now that Susan has had to struggle to remember the details. It was certainly never a topic of discussion in her family; somehow all of the children knew better than to ever bring it up.

Susan's mother has seemed to be doing well for the past ten years, although Susan has not had much more than annual contact with her and therefore cannot determine what factors have played a role in her improvement. These days she talks enthusiastically about her retirement in a warm climate, which has allowed her to take long walks and swim almost every day. The last time she saw her mother, Susan felt confident about her because she looked healthy and happy and seemed to enjoy being outdoors so much.

Susan's father, who had worked hard as a store manager and was well liked, had died of a heart attack when she was twenty-five. In describing him, Susan reported that he was cheerful and fun-loving, not a depressed type at all. His only vice was that he chain-smoked cigarettes and yes, he enjoyed his beer and whiskey. On the other hand, whenever he seemed angry or sad, he would head down to the neighborhood tavern and get drunk. Luckily, he lived close enough to the bar to stagger the two blocks home at closing time. Susan remembered her mother worrying about his drinking too much, but her father assured her that drinking was a harmless part of his family culture. Besides, he only got drunk twice a month or so. "Big deal," he would say. "A fellow needs to tie one on once in a while to get through life." When she was growing up, Susan would never have considered her father an alcoholic. Now, knowing more about the criteria for alcoholism, she would have to say that he probably did have a problem with alcohol that often masked symptoms of depression—although her father surely would have denied it.

Susan never knew her grandparents on her father's side; but she had strong impressions of her maternal grandparents, and their moods, from her mother and from her own memories as a child. She thought of her maternal grandfather as a "whirlwind" who woke up early, did many chores, and was very active most of the time working as a carpenter. He seemed very even-tempered and although a little distant, did not suffer from moodiness or depression. Susan remembers her grandmother also as full of energy and active, and sometimes overly excitable. But she also had her moody spells, when everyone knew not to bother her, when she was despairing and depressed. Then she would snap out of them, and was full of grand plans and activity until her moodiness returned and her plans seemed unattainable. Her mood swings sounded very much like those of manic-depressive illness. However, they seemed to be mild to moderate, as she was never hospitalized.

In Susan's generation, her brother has suffered the most severe symptoms of depression, her sister seems to have been spared the disease, and Susan is herself suffering relatively mild symptoms that could intensify if left untreated. This family profile is a typical one of families with a genetic predisposition to depression.

How do you know if you or your family is at risk for depression? In chapter 2, there is a self-test and a full explanation of the key factors in determining the inheritance of the genetic predisposition for depressive illness.

The Environmental Component

Even if you find that you *have* inherited this predisposition, it doesn't mean that you're doomed to be depressed. Many people who are born with the susceptibility to depression never experience any of the symptoms. We are the product of our genes, but we are also the product of our environment. Environmental factors play a key role in whether your vulnerability to depression will actually result in the illness, and can also be significant enough in themselves to cause depression.

Which environmental factors play a role? Just about all of those that affect the quality of our lives, including:

- Relationships with family and friends.
- Physical and mental health.
- Financial and employment security/satisfaction.
- Satisfaction with your life situation.
- Ability to pursue pleasurable activities.

Perhaps the most important environmental factors, however, are stressful events that we are confronted with in our lives, and the ways in which we cope with those stresses. Any major change can be considered a stressful event, including moving, job changes, vacations, marriages, births, divorces, deaths, even anniversaries and holidays such as Christmas. Each of us has a different ability to cope with stress, and we are better at dealing with some types than others. If the environmental stress becomes greater than we are capable of handling at a given time, *particularly* if there is a family history of depression, then depression can be the result.

For example, Bob is usually a happy, active person who handles his responsibilities as a father, husband, and fire fighter well. While he does have a genetic predisposition to depression, Bob has always remained symptom-free. However, six months ago a series of events combined to overload his capacity for handling stress. Within a six-month period, Bob hurt his back and was bedridden for two months, his father died unexpectedly, and he had serious arguments with his wife about their vacation plans. He seemed to be handling all of this fairly well until one day when his car was stolen. This random event seemed to push him over the edge, and with the loss of his car, he became inconsolable. Bob began having many of the symptoms of depression: insomnia, feelings of despondency and hopelessness, loss of self-esteem, and a lack of interest in things he once enjoyed. He withdrew from the world and his family by spending his days sleeping and his nights at the local bar, where he got drunk on a daily basis. However, when Bob finally turned to Alcoholics Anonymous for help, it became clear that underneath the problem of alcoholism lurked depression. Subsequently, Bob was successfully treated with antidepressant medication and psychotherapy. He now is aware of his vulnerability to depression, and he uses preventive measures to combat his predisposition, including a regimen of steady exercise.

Much of the time, we are unable to control the stresses that come our way, but we should be aware that too much stress can push us over the edge, as it did with Bob. Furthermore, we can attempt to control our environment to minimize stress and to arrange supports when we recognize that the stress is more than we can handle alone.

Your mental attitude—the way in which you perceive the world and yourself—plays an important role in fighting your vulnerability toward depression. Having a genetic disposition toward depression does not doom you to a life of depression. You should not live in constant fear that there is something looming over your head, ready to drop down at you at any moment. This book is meant to point you toward awareness, education, treatment, and prevention. Together, they will allow you to beat the odds and prevent your predisposition from turning into depressive illness.

2

The Genetic Factor in Depression

How can you find out if depression runs in your family? First, you will need to gather as much information concerning depression in your family history as you can. The best way to organize this information so that it will be useful to you is through construction of your own family genogram.

What is a genogram? It is a diagram of your family tree with information about family members and their relationships over several generations. Genograms typically focus on different kinds of information, such as family dynamics, medical histories, or occupations, to help clinicians map social relationships within the family. The focus of your genogram is the prevalence of depression and other mental illness in your family.

How to Create Your Family's Genogram

The frame of a genogram is a pictorial depiction of how different family members are biologically related to one another across several generations. Genograms are most useful if they cover at least three generations, so begin by drawing a diagram that puts your generation at the bottom, then your parents' and grandparents' generations above yours. The standard genogram symbols, described in *Genograms in Family Assessment* by Monica McGoldrick and Randy Gerson (W. W. Norton & Co., 1985), are as follows:

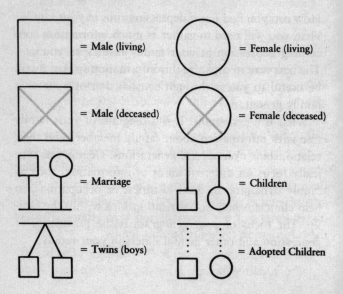

= Male (living)   = Female (living)

= Male (deceased)   = Female (deceased)

= Marriage   = Children

= Twins (boys)   = Adopted Children

Vertical lines connect married couples, with their children listed below (oldest to youngest from left to right). With these basic symbols, you can draw your family structure on a genogram. Draw a double line around the symbol for yourself to distinguish it on the diagram. We will diagram Susan's family using the information in chapter 1 as an example.

Before you begin to draw the actual genogram, it is helpful to keep a separate record of your findings as you gather facts about your family's history, as it may take some time and research to obtain details about earlier generations. Talk to as many family members as you can to get an accurate picture of the incidence of depression in your family. Don't give up if some details aren't perfectly clear: a partial genogram is helpful too.

First record the year of birth and death for each person, then fill in information relevant to your search for the history of depression in your family: was anyone treated for depression? did they have frequent or infrequent depressive episodes? were any family members suspected of being depressed? Suicide attempts should also be indicated, as this behavior is linked to depression. In addition to determining heredity, some therapists also use genograms to record patterns of relationships within a family to help understand the dynamics of a person's emotional relationships. In this case, the therapist would also ask you to record such information as separation, divorce, couples who are living together but not married, and love affairs. This is the information table for Susan's family:

SUSAN'S GENERATION: Susan b. '55; brother Matt b. '50 (hospitalized, suicide attempts '74, '78); sister Pam b. '49

PARENTS: **Mother**—Edna b. '30 (several depressive episodes; one of four children, one of brothers was alcoholic)

Father—George b. '29, d. '80 of heart attack (alcoholism problem, one of six children, one of brothers had nervous breakdown and was hospitalized for depression)

GRANDPARENTS: Maternal grandmother—Clarissa b. '10, d. '75 (mild manic-depressive symptoms)

Maternal grandfather—Henry b. '08, d. '73 (very active)

Paternal grandmother—Ruth b. '08, d. '80 (unhappy and fearful—possible depression)

Paternal grandfather—Charles b. '06, d. '66 (possible alcoholic)

Using this information, we have constructed Susan's family genogram on page 23.

Looking at Susan's family genogram, we can clearly see that depression is found in all three generations and alcoholism in two.

You should be able to draw your family genogram with similar information. This amount of information is the minimum you need for a useful genogram. For your own interest you might want to include other information such as physical illnesses or addictions. If you know more facts about family members that might be interesting, it can be useful to indicate the occupation or any other unique characteristics.

Using the information from your family genogram, you can now take the Genetic Risk Self-Test.

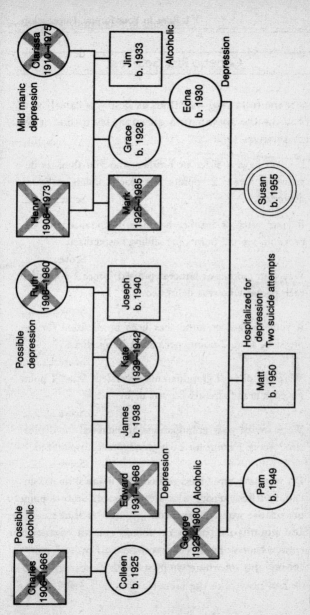

Figure 1. Susan's Genogram.

Genetic Risk Self-Test

Answer the following questions as best you can. If you don't know the answer to a question, try to find it by asking relatives.

1. Do you have a sister or brother who you think is depressed? Score 2 points for each sibling who is depressed.   Score_____

2. If your sister or brother has been hospitalized for depression, score 2 points per sibling hospitalized.
                                                           Score_____

3. Was your mother or father depressed? Score 2 points for each parent who was depressed.
                                                           Score_____

4. If your mother or father has been hospitalized for depression, score 2 points per parent hospitalized.
                                                           Score_____

5. Were any of your grandparents depressed? Score 1 point for each grandparent who was depressed.
                                                           Score_____

6. Were any of your grandparents hospitalized for depression? Score 1 point for each grandparent hospitalized.
                                                           Score_____

7. Do you have any blood-related (not in-laws) aunts, uncles, and first cousins who are depressed? Score 1 point per relative who is depressed.   Score_____

8. Did any of your parents or siblings attempt to commit suicide because he or she was depressed? Score 2 points for each person who attempted suicide.
                                                           Score_____

9. Would you consider any of your parents or siblings to have a problem with alcoholism? Score 1 point for each close relative with alcoholism.

Score_____

10. If your score on the Depression Self-Test (page 00) was 0–7, add 0 points; 8–15, 2 points; 16–25, 4 points; 26–30, 6 points.   Score_____

SCORING: 0–2: Your risk is minimal.
            2–5: You have moderate risk.
            5–8: You have high risk.
            8 up: Your risk is very high.

Now that you have some sense of your personal risk, it's necessary to understand why the risk factors are so important. Scientists and mental health professionals first began to suspect that depression might be inherited because of its prevalence among family members. The evidence suggested strongly that there might be a genetic component, but some were not convinced that it was the genes and not the environment. If your grandmother, mother, sister, and cousin all suffered from depression, how do we know that it wasn't a *learned* family trait? Are families capable of acquiring similar personality styles without necessarily having been *born* with them? The evidence points to a strong genetic component.

Let's look at the evidence: Several research studies of identical twins examined the question of whether depression could be inherited. Identical twin studies have been very useful in studying the inheritance of traits because identical twins have the exact same genetic makeup. Research studies on identical twins separated from birth can look at whether specific traits of twins are similar (suggesting the effect of inherited genes) or different (suggesting the effect of their different environments).

The identical twin studies first provided strong evidence that nature, rather than nurture (or genes rather than the environment), was responsible for depressive illness. Data showed that if one identical twin suffers from depression, the likelihood that the other identical twin also will ranges from *40 to 70 percent*. For nonidentical twins (also known as fraternal twins) who share similar social environments while growing up, the likelihood is much lower. Instead, the likelihood that if one fraternal twin suffers from depression, the other twin will too, is only *0 to 13 percent*. This likelihood is the same as for any two (nontwin) siblings.

The most fascinating information from the twin studies was found with identical twins who were raised apart from each other because of adoption at birth. These studies demonstrated that when identical twins are raised apart, the likelihood that both twins would suffer from depression is exactly the same as that of identical twins who had been raised together. In other words, while the twins' social environments may have been totally different, their genetic makeups were the same. This finding proved to be convincing evidence that inheritance plays a major role in the susceptibility toward depression.

Other studies of adopted children also point to the

strong influence of genes in being at risk for depression. Adopted children whose biological parents suffered from depressive mood disorders were compared with adopted children whose biological parents did *not*. Results indicated that the first group of children were significantly more likely to develop symptoms of depression than the second group. Dr. Gershon of the National Institute of Mental Health reported that in a group of depressed adoptive children, 30 percent of their biological parents suffered from depression while only 2 percent of their adoptive parents suffered from depression. This finding indicates that the inherited genetic risk of depression is greater than the environmental risk of living with an adoptive parent who may be depressed.

While there is no genetic proof yet that unipolar depression is inherited, studies such as these point to a strong genetic link for depression. Keep in mind that environment is still a cofactor of the risk of depression. In fact, it is widely accepted that risk for depression is created by an interaction between nature and nurture, or between your genes and your environment.

There is compelling evidence that indicates that manic-depressive illness, also known as bipolar disorder, is inherited. A decade-long study of the Amish of Lancaster County, Pennsylvania, has not only established conclusive statistical evidence of the inheritance of manic-depression, but claims to have linked cases of it in an Amish family to the genes found in a specific region of human chromosome 11. How this was accomplished is a fascinating tale of medical detective work. The Old Amish Order of Lancaster County is an isolated community into which very few outsiders have married for two hundred years. The incidence of manic-depressive illness is no higher among the Amish than in the general population. But because of their limited gene pool, they were an ideal sample population to study. In addition, because the Amish have maintained their own customs and strict social conventions for two centuries, the consistent environment minimizes the effect of non-genetic influences in the development of mood disorders.

Manic-depressive behavior, characterized by mood swings between loud, show-off behavior and despon-dent, hopeless depression stands out like a sore thumb in this quiet, hardworking community. So it was easy for the researchers to identify those Amish who suffered from this illness.

Finally, the Amish have kept careful genealogical re-cords that date back to the arrival of the community's original twenty to thirty families from Europe in the 1700s. These genealogical records precisely document the line of inheritance for every individual within the Amish community.

The researchers, headed by Dr. Janice Egeland of the University of Miami School of Medicine, identified thirty-two individuals (approximately 2 percent of the total community) in the Old Amish Order who were suffering from manic-depression. When genograms of these thirty-two individuals were consulted, it was found that all of them had family histories of the illness back through several generations, providing strong cir-cumstantial evidence for the inheritability of the disease. Even more remarkable, the results strongly suggest an inherited susceptibility to suicidal behavior. Because of their strict religious beliefs against suicide, the suicide rate among the Amish is much lower than in the general population. Since 1880, there have been only twenty-six suicides recorded. However, the researchers were amazed to find that all of the twenty-six suicides occurred within only four families—clearly not a coincidence.

The researchers then focused on one eighty-one-member family clan. Manic-depressive illness was diagnosed in fourteen members of this family; five other members were found to be suffering severe depression. After the researchers had obtained blood samples from each member of the clan, they isolated the DNA from each sample. When gene segments from the manic-depressive individuals were compared with those from normal family members, they found that two genes at the tip of chromosome 11 appeared together only in those Amish with diagnoses of manic-depressive illness. Given these results, the scientists concluded that a gene or a number of genes in the region of chromosome 11 may result in the inheritance of a predisposition to manic-depressive illness. Some consider this finding a major scientific breakthrough in the search for the *gene markers* of manic-depression. There is no *conclusive* evidence, however, that proves that the depression-related genes are found on any one particular chromosome site.

The researchers also believe that the gene is a dominant one, that is, the inheritance of it from either parent can give an individual a predisposition to manic-depression. They claim that children of an individual with this unusual genetic makeup have a 50 percent chance of inheriting the gene. However, inheriting this gene anomaly only *predisposes* a child to the illness, and does not guarantee manic-depression itself. Only 63 percent of those carrying the manic-depressive gene actually demonstrate the illness. As mentioned previously, environmental factors (explored in the next chapter) and perhaps the interaction of other genetic traits, such as traits for mental illnesses like schizophrenia, also seem to play important roles in determining whether a susceptible individual will ultimately suffer from the disease.

While these exciting findings seem to offer compelling evidence, other studies have failed to find the same chromosomal structure in non-Amish manic-depressives. Researchers have not been discouraged, however; they suggest that more than one gene may be responsible for the predisposition to manic-depression. The U.S. government, recognizing the importance of genetic testing, designated $62 million in 1989 to finance the Human Genome Project and pledged another $3 billion to continue this work over the next fifteen years. There are 50,000 to 100,000 individual genes that together make up the human genome; the goal of the collaboration of genetics researchers on the Human Genome Project is to locate and identify each of them and to decode the information they contain. With a more complete understanding of genes and how they are inherited and expressed, science may be able to determine with certainty what now can only be guessed about hereditary diseases.

Scientists hope that one day they will be able to take a blood or tissue sample from a baby, analyze his or her DNA structure, and be able to tell the parents what this child's risk is for depression and other mental and physical illnesses. Until such biochemical diagnosis is developed, however, individuals can still assess their risk for manic-depression and depression through their family histories by measuring the incidence of mood disorders in their relatives. The evidence points to a genetic basis for depression; that is, a predisposition for depression is clearly inherited through one's genetic makeup. Therefore, this family background information will help people to predict whether their children will be at risk for depression; and awareness, active prevention, and early treatment may be able to save many individuals from suffering unnecessary misery.

Some Common Questions About Genetic Aspects of Depression

Q: Depression has been diagnosed in someone in my family. I know I'm probably at higher risk for getting depressed, but how much higher is it?

A: If one family member has depressive or manic-depressive illness, the risk of the illness among first-degree family relatives (children, parents, and siblings) is *two* to *three* times higher than average.

Q: My mother and my brother both suffer from depression. What are the chances that I or one of my siblings will also develop depressive illness?

A: If one parent and one child have an affective mood disorder such as depression, any other child in the family has a 25 percent (or 1 in 4) chance of developing the same disorder.

Q: Does the risk increase if *both* parents have depressive illness?

A: Definitely. If *both* parents *and* one child in the family have depressive illness, other children in the family have a 40 percent chance of being depressed.

Q: Are there other factors that affect the risk of inheriting depression?

A: Yes. The *earlier* the onset of depression in an individual, the greater the risk for major depression developing in his or her relatives. If an individual suffers a first major depression *before* the age of twenty, his or her relatives have a higher risk than if it had developed later. While it's not always easy, be sure to find out when a depressed family member first exhibited the symptoms. The younger the relative was, the *greater* your risk for depression.

Other factors that *increase* your risk are:

- The presence of an anxiety disorder (extreme anxiety over commonplace events).
- A history of *alcoholism* in the family.

Q: Why is alcoholism a risk factor?

A: The rate of depression in families of alcoholics is significantly *greater* than in the general population. One explanation is that alcoholism often masks the symptoms of depression because frequently depressed individuals use alcohol to ease the pain. Then when alcoholism is diagnosed, the possible underlying cause—depression—may be missed.

(This is not to imply that all alcoholics suffer from depression.)

Q: If there is a "depressed gene," are depressed parents the only ones who carry the depression? Do nondepressed parents play a role in passing the gene along to their children?

A: Recent studies have suggested that both depressed and nondepressed parents can carry and pass along depression-linked genes to their offspring. However, the fact that nondepressed adults may be carriers of these genes indicates that genetics gives you only a predisposition or vulnerability to the disorder. If this is the case, then there certainly are individuals who have inherited the vulnerability, and may pass it on to their children, without themselves exhibiting any symptoms.

Q: Aren't there many ways in which families are depressed that have nothing to do with genes? Could families pass on depression because of the way they interact with each other?

A: Family interaction and socialization clearly play important roles in whether depression will be passed on between generations. Environmental factors, such as situational stresses and events, also can make a difference in whether family members will suffer from depression. Environmental factors seem to determine whether the seed (the genetic predisposition) that is already there will grow and bloom.

Q: Is the risk of inheriting some types of depression higher than for others?

A: Yes. Two types of depression seem to be inherited

more often. They are *major endogenous depression* and *manic-depression* (see page 6). The risk of inheriting these is higher than for other, more moderate, forms of depression.

Q: Is the risk for inheriting depression higher or lower for different racial groups?

A: The risk for the genetic inheritance of depression seems to be the same across racial groups. However, the incidence of depression may be higher among some racial/ethnic groups than others because of environmental factors. (See chapter 7.)

Q: What about male and female differences? Is the risk for inheriting depression higher for men or for women?

A: Evidence indicates that the overall risk seems to be the same for both men and women. However, since the incidence of *diagnosed* depression is more than two times as high for women as for men, there has been a great deal of speculation that the chance of inheriting depression was twice as high for women. This theory focused on the X chromosome. If the gene for depression is located on the X chromosome, and the trait is dominant, females, who have two X chromosomes, would have twice the opportunity to be affected by depression than would males, who have only one X chromosome. In addition, if this theory was correct, males could inherit the depression gene from their mothers only, not from their fathers (males get one X chromosome from their mothers and one Y chromosome from their fathers).

The results of family studies have not been conclusive, but a 1985 study looked at this question by examining data on more than 1,000 first-degree relatives of 133 depressed individuals. The results indicated that the gender of the depressed person was not a factor in the transmission of depression. Relatives of male and female depressed persons had equal rates of depression. Furthermore, there were many documented cases of depression that seemed clearly to have been passed on from father to son. These results showed that depression was not linked to the X chromosome.

Thus, other factors must be responsible for the increased prevalence of depression among women. In fact, even if there is no genetic risk, serious forms of the disease can still afflict you (although the chances are much lower compared to cases in which a genetic predisposition exists). In chapter 3, we will examine some of these factors.

You now have the results of the Genetic Risk Self-Test (in the beginning of this chapter) and have created your family genogram to measure your own risk for inheriting the predisposition for depression. So you're probably wondering if there's anything you can do to reduce your risk. Now that you have this information about your family and your own risk, please remember that you've measured only a predisposition for depression. Having a predisposition does not mean that you are destined to be depressed in your lifetime.

If your family has this predisposition, you need to work on prevention and to get early treatment to control the vulnerability. Ignoring your risk potential, hoping it will go away, or not discussing it with others (either family members or mental health professionals) because you feel ashamed will not decrease the risk. If your risk potential is high, don't keep it a secret. Tell your sisters and brothers, parents, cousins, aunts, uncles, and, by all means, your children (if they are old enough) what their risk is.

This chapter explained that your vulnerability to depression is not a character flaw or your own personal problem. It is a family problem that you may have been born with. There is nothing to be embarrassed or ashamed of. In fact, many clinicians report that people who have been feeling depressed and have been blaming themselves are relieved to find out about the inheritability of depression. Instead of personalizing the problems and wondering what they did wrong in their lives, they understand that depression has genetic and biological roots much like other illnesses such as diabetes or high blood pressure. And like those other illnesses, there are steps that you can take to decrease your risk.

There is actually much that you can do to help yourself and your family understand, prevent, and treat depressive illness. First, show your relatives your family genogram. Inform others in your family about their increased risk of inheriting depression. Have them take the Genetic Risk Self-Test in this chapter and the Depression Self-Test in chapter 1, and tell them that they, like you, can take charge of the situation. You can make a big difference by working on preventing depression and receiving early, effective treatment.

Remember, only 20 percent of depression is diagnosed and treated correctly. The treatment for depression is now quite effective, but you must first acknowledge the problem. In the chapters ahead, I will address how environmental factors play a role, and how you can optimize your environment, learn about prevention, and get early, appropriate treatment for symptoms of depression.

3

Environmental Factors and Stresses

Depression is a widespread, common illness that strikes people no matter what their class, race, age, gender, marital status, or education. Statistics tell us that 1 out of every 5 people will suffer from moderate to serious depression in their lifetime. No one is sheltered from the risk of depression because of financial security, success, or age, but some environmental factors do put you at *more* risk than others.

We already know that some people are at higher risk for depression because of their genetic background. However, there are other risk factors that are not inherited, but are individual risk factors. These include:

- Maladaptive family patterns of interaction.
- Early loss of a nurturing relationship.
- Stressful life events.
- Lack of social support.
- Negative attitude and personality style.

Since depression is an illness that is caused by a mix of your biological/genetic makeup, life experience, and personality style, these psychosocial factors play an important role in determining whether you will become depressed.

Let's examine each of the five risk factors so that you can rate your own personal risk for each factor.

Factor 1:
Maladaptive Family Patterns of Interaction

In chapter 2, we focused on the increased risk of depression for those whose family genograms showed a history of depression. The explanation for the increased risk was the transmission of "depressed-related genes" that predisposed individuals to this illness. Beyond genetics, however, it is reasonable to assume that there is a strong *environmental* impact of having a close relative with depression (or indeed, any serious psychiatric or physical illness), which would affect the family dynamics and interaction. The results may not be apparent while a child is growing up, but could increase his or her potential for depression in adulthood nevertheless. Whether the impact is evident early on or not, parental depression can definitely affect a child.

Since children identify with their parents, they learn how to react to situations by modeling their parents' behavior. If a child sees her depressed mother react to a stressful situation by withdrawing, she will tend to act the same way when confronted with similar situations. For example, Pauline, six, does well in school but has trouble playing with others during recess. Whenever there is a struggle over playground equipment, such as fighting for use of a swing or a ball, she gives up easily. And instead of playing with something else, Pauline runs to her "safe spot," a bench near the playground monitor, and sits by herself for several minutes, gathering up the courage to return to play. When Pauline was two years old, her mother was in a car accident and became depressed enough to be hospitalized for a short time. Since that incident, her mother has avoided going out. Whenever there is any sign of major conflict or stress in her interpersonal relationships, Pauline's mother tries to avoid dealing with it by withdrawing to her home or going to her own mother's home. She prefers to let her husband handle all the difficulties in their family's life. Even at the young age of six, Pauline has learned from her mother that the world can be a dangerous place when there is stress or conflict, and she tries her best to avoid it.

If you had a depressed parent or other relative who spent significant amounts of time with you, you may have learned some of his or her behaviors, or you may have inherited some behavioral traits—or both. Try to remember if they had poor coping skills, were easily overwhelmed, or seemed overly helpless. If this type of behavior was present in your family, you have a higher risk for depression.

Factor 2:
Early Loss of a Nurturing
Relationship

The association between the early loss of an important nurturing caretaker (such as a parent) and depression was first introduced by the founder of psychoanalysis, Sigmund Freud, in 1917. He theorized that adult depression is a person's reaction to a perceived loss that reawakens depressive feelings associated with the earlier loss of a parent by death or separation. In other words, things that happen in a person's life repeat themselves, so you are at a higher risk for depression if you suffered a loss earlier in your life. To this day, Freud's theory is still believed by many psychologists. Research evidence is conflicting, but some studies do support this theory, at least in part. One study found that 25 percent of a sample of clinically depressed patients had a history of discernible loss or separation, as compared to only 5 to 10 percent of a similar group of nondepressed individuals.

In looking at possible causes of depression, loss and separation are important factors that may increase the relative risk of some people. It is likely that the timing of the loss or separation may determine its seriousness. If the loss occurs at a crucial developmental stage, or at a time when an individual is particularly vulnerable, its role in increasing the potential for depression becomes greater. Let's look at another example:

David is a four-year-old who attends preschool for 5 hours a day. His teachers have been complaining about his behavior because he is aggressive and often fights with other children. When David was eighteen months old, his father left the family and has had no contact with David since then. David frequently claims that he doesn't like the other kids in his preschool class and wants to stay with his mother instead of going to preschool.

In David's situation, it is too early to say whether his loss at the age of eighteen months will increase his potential for depression as an adult. However, his current behavior indicates that he's having some social adjustment problems that might well be related to the loss of his father. Depression takes different forms for children than for adults. It is not unusual for a depressed nursery school child to act out in an aggressive manner, rather than to withdraw. As a child, David can only convey his unhappiness and low sense of self-esteem through his aggressive behavior and his desire to remain home with his mother. He is a child who is suffering from his own symptoms of depression now, and both he and his mother would benefit from psychotherapy. Treatment might involve helping him to acknowledge his unhappiness, accept the loss of his father, understand how this is a difficult time for him, and express his feelings in a more appropriate manner. Any treatment would certainly need to include David's mother to enlist her help and to offer her support and guidance in David's care.

Another example is the case of Jackie, twenty-nine, whose mother died suddenly when she was only three years old. Cared for by her father and a grandmother,

Jackie felt she had a reasonably happy childhood. By most standards, she has been quite successful, with a satisfying marriage, children, and a promising career as a college professor. When her father died of cancer two years ago, Jackie was upset but felt she handled his death well. She went back to work the day after his funeral. Yet recently she had begun to feel an emptiness and a sadness that would not abate. When Jackie entered psychotherapy to cope with her strong feelings of sadness, she found that she needed to grieve not only for the loss of her father, but also for her mother. Growing up, Jackie had heard very little about her mother, almost as if she had never existed, because her family did not want her to miss her. As a result, she had never really come to terms with how devastating her mother's death was in her life. When Jackie's father died, her bereavement was also shortened and she became quite depressed two years after his death. After Jackie allowed herself to grieve and mourn the loss of both of her parents, her depression lifted.

It is common, even expected, for most people to become depressed after a loved one has died. This bereavement process usually lasts up to a year. Over this period of time, the individual's acute sense of loss and pain gradually subsides, and the symptoms of depression slowly dissipate. However, for some individuals, the acute depression, pain, and sadness continue far beyond a year's time. If the depression continues without abatement for over a year, it can indicate a more serious depression that was precipitated by the loss of a loved one.

Paradoxically, if an individual fails to fully acknowledge the feelings about the loss, and does not go through a complete bereavement process, as in Jackie's case, he or she may suffer from prolonged depression at some future point.

So, as you can see, if you have experienced a loss of a parent or other important caretaker during your childhood, you may be at higher risk for depression in adulthood.

Factor 3:
Stressful Life Events

Psychological studies provide strong evidence that people who are depressed have experienced a greater number of stressful life events before the onset of their depression than have nondepressed persons during this same time period. What are stressful life events? Well, different things are stressful for different people, but there is general agreement that change, whether for better or worse, is stressful.

How can you measure the stress in your own life? Use the Stress Scale. Developed at the University of Washington medical school by Drs. Thomas H. Holmes and Richard H. Rahe in 1965, the Stress Scale assigns various scores to a number of life changes, both positive and negative. By measuring how stressful your life has been in the past twelve months, you can rate your own risk for depression and illness. Note that Holmes and Rahe consider it a scale for *illness,* not specifically depression. Clearly, physical and mental illness are interrelated, and to be at risk for depression correlates with an increase in risk for physical illness as well.

Stress Scale*

To find your score, check the events applying to you during the past twelve months. Then add up the total values.

Rank	Event	Value	Your Score
1	Death of spouse	100	_____
2	Divorce	73	_____
3	Marital separation	65	_____
4	Jail term	63	_____
5	Death of close family member	63	_____
6	Personal injury or illness	53	_____
7	Marriage	50	_____
8	Fired from work	47	_____
9	Marital reconciliation	45	_____
10	Retirement	45	_____
11	Change in family member's health	44	_____
12	Pregnancy	40	_____
13	Sex difficulties	39	_____
14	Addition to family	39	_____
15	Business readjustment	39	_____
16	Change in financial status	38	_____
17	Death of close friend	37	_____
18	Change to different line of work	36	_____
19	Change in number of marital arguments	35	_____
20	Major mortgage or loan	31	_____
21	Foreclosure of mortgage or loan	30	_____
22	Change in work responsibilities	29	_____

Rank	Event	Value	Your Score
23	Son or daughter leaving home	29	_____
24	Trouble with in-laws	29	_____
25	Outstanding personal achievement	28	_____
26	Spouse begins or stops work	26	_____
27	Starting or finishing school	26	_____
28	Change in living conditions	25	_____
29	Revision of personal habits	24	_____
30	Trouble with boss	23	_____
31	Change in work hours, conditions	20	_____
32	Change in residence	20	_____
33	Change in schools	20	_____
34	Change in recreational habits	19	_____
35	Change in church activities	19	_____
36	Change in social activities	18	_____
37	Minor mortgage or loan	17	_____
38	Change in sleeping habits	16	_____
39	Change in number of family gatherings	15	_____
40	Change in eating habits	15	_____
41	Vacation	13	_____
42	Christmas season	12	_____
43	Minor violation of the law	11	_____
TOTAL			_____

*Used with permission.

What do the scores mean? If your score is above 300, you are at high risk for depression and other illnesses.

If your score is between 150 and 299, you are at moderate risk for depression and illness. If your score is below 150, your stress level is relatively low and should not be a factor in your risk for depression and illness.

Can this scale be used to measure a child's stressful life events? Yes, but it would obviously need some modification, with stronger emphasis on some changes than others. With children, it is important for parents (who are often overwhelmed themselves) to be aware of the increased stress that moving, vacations, deaths, etc., place on a child who has even less control over his or her life than adults do. Children also have fewer resources to cope with changes.

Vicki, five, is an example of a young child whose parents have moved three times in three years. Her parents didn't think it affected her very much because she was not yet attending school. Yet no sooner did she become accustomed to one location, when they moved again. During this time period, Vicki's appetite decreased, she refused to sleep in her room alone, and she spent as much time as she was allowed watching the same Winnie the Pooh videotape over and over. It was not until her parents recognized the signs of depression in Vicki that they received some professional help from a child therapist. Gradually, Vicki's enthusiasm for food returned, as did her ability to sleep alone and have fun with other children. The effect of changes in a young child's life can easily go unnoticed. Behavior changes that may seem unrelated to stress can be prevented if parents are more sensitive to how stressful life events can affect their children.

While this Stress Scale assigns weighted scores for

events that are considered stressful for most people in general, there are specific events that are more stressful at different ages and stages of development. Studies have found that college students are more depressed than the general population of young adults at that age. Recent surveys of students at four universities found that 25 percent of the enrolled students suffered some symptoms of depression at any one time, and as many as 75 percent of the students reported being depressed at some point over the past school year. Three groups of life events seemed to be particularly stressful for students: (1) changes in a living situation, (2) the need to define goals for life and career, and (3) feelings of alienation and loneliness.

Let's look at Donna as an example. Donna's problems were not unusual, but her response to them was. She was a nineteen-year-old freshman living at a university. Having done well in high school, she had expected to perform reasonably well in college.

But academic work was more demanding than Donna had anticipated. Instead of pursuing extracurricular activities she used to enjoy, she devoted much of her time to studying. Since her parents were sacrificing to allow her to attend college, she felt she owed it to them to do her very best. Her first semester exam results were excellent, but Donna didn't feel relieved. Instead, she feared that she could not keep up this relentless task of studying every spare minute. Donna began to eat less and less, canceling her meal plan in her dormitory. She lost ten pounds in three months. Since she was studying all the time, she made no new friends and had no one to share her problems with.

Using the money saved from her meals, Donna decided that she would try to ease the financial burden on her parents. She began to travel to Atlantic City on weekends to gamble. The first two times she won some money, but the third time she had a streak of bad luck and lost it all. Donna felt so despondent and depressed she couldn't bring herself to return to school. She did, however, call her roommate and explain the situation. Luckily, her roommate alerted university counseling personnel who were able to contact Donna and persuade her to receive help. This story has a happy ending, as Donna was able to recognize her feelings of depression, understand the loneliness, and began to better cope with the stressful events that had changed her life.

Not all college students are as lucky as Donna in getting the help that they need. Many students have a very difficult time adjusting to the stressful events in their lives. But if they receive the support that they need, students have a better chance of making the adjustment.

Factor 4:
Lack of Social Support

A recent study of depression among college students conducted by Mary Kay O'Neil, Ph.D, William Lancee, M.S.C., and Stanley Freeman, M.D., at the University of Toronto, found that the presence of social support, almost always in the form of a confidant, was the most important factor in determining whether a student became depressed or not. A confidant is a friend who meets all of the following criteria: (1) he or she is easily available; (2) he or she is someone with whom even the most personal difficulties can be shared; and (3) he or she is someone with whom the confiding relationship is reciprocal. For college students, having a confidant seems to work as a guard against depression.

Not only is having a confidant a positive factor, in some age groups, it is crucial. In fact, for college students, the *absence* of a confidant, even when stressful life events were *not* present, *increased* the risk for depressive symptoms. Research has shown that for older adults, social support is most necessary when they experience a high level of stressful events. However, because college students are in a transitional state between their families of origin and their own future families, they are still in the process of establishing their own support system.

To have a confidant during this transitional time provides a sense of stability and self-confidence. Having a confidant also alleviates the sense of aloneness, that feeling of alienation reported by people who are depressed. In times of high stress a confidant can help you to cope successfully with life's hardships.

Mark is an example of a person in his early twenties who went through a transitional period when he enlisted in the navy. All of a sudden he found himself across the country from his family and friends. His basic training was demanding and Mark was always surrounded by plenty of people, but he felt very lonely. A quiet, shy person, Mark had had one or two friends during high school, and it had always taken him a long time to warm up to people. Mark was very close to his parents and felt comfortable talking to them about almost everything in his life. His parents seemed to have played the role of confidant.

Now that he was assigned to a ship, however, Mark had no opportunity to communicate with his parents except by letter. It was a new and very frustrating experience to be completely on his own. He saw that most of his fellow shipmates had become fast and easy friends with each other, but he lacked the self-confidence or ability to make new friends. The other cadets thought that Mark was aloof or distant and pretty much left him alone.

Lacking a confidant, Mark withdrew further and further into himself. He found it difficult to concentrate on his tasks during the day because he was so unhappy. When his work performance began to slip, Mark was reprimanded by his superior officer. During their meeting, Mark cried and admitted that he was very lonely and depressed. He asked to be discharged from the navy.

Eventually, Mark was discharged, but not before he received a psychological evaluation that found that he was suffering from many symptoms of clinical depression, some of which probably derived from a genetic predisposition. Navy psychologists recommended that Mark be involved in a group counseling situation to help him learn basic social skills, skills that would help him to form a relationship with a confidant one day.

You may be better at making friends than Mark was, but do you currently have a confidant? If you have a genetic predisposition to depression and you don't have another available person with whom you can share your difficulties, then you are also at an *increased* risk for depression. The risk is even higher if you don't have a confidant *and* it's a stressful time in your life.

Factor 5:
Negative Attitude and Personality Style

Several psychological theories have been developed to explain why and how people become depressed. These theories not only help to explain behavior but also serve as guidelines in treating depression. The three major psychological theories will be discussed in this book.

The first, the *learned helplessness* theory, was developed by Dr. Martin Seligman. While doing research on animal and human responses to stressful situations, Seligman was surprised to find that people reacted just as animals did when he exposed them to the same unpleasant experiences. When animals such as dogs and goats were exposed to a loud noise that continued no matter what they tried to do to make it stop, they soon gave up. They acted completely helpless. Even when the conditions were changed and the animals could stop the noise, most of them didn't try. They seem to have resigned themselves to not having any control and given up. The same behavior was seen in people who were exposed to a loud noise: after a while, the people gave up and began to show symptoms of depression—helplessness and loss of self-esteem in response to losing control over the situation.

This idea of learned helplessness helps to explain how people give up because they learn that no matter what they do, nothing will change a bad situation, and depression is the result.

Over time, Seligman and his colleagues found that their theory did not apply to all situations. There were times when exposure to uncontrollable bad events did *not* lead to helplessness and depression in some individuals. The theory also did not explain the loss of self-esteem and self-confidence often seen in depressed people. In general, people don't usually blame themselves for events or situations over which they have no real control. If learned helplessness could not explain why some people became depressed, were there other factors that made them more susceptible than others?

In a revised theory, Seligman emphasized attitude, or what he calls "explanatory style" to describe why some people get depressed while others don't under the same bad circumstances. People don't just accept events uncritically; they usually ask *why* things happen the way they do. And the answer, or the explanation that they give for why the event happened to them, affects what they expect about the future. That explanation will also determine the extent to which they will be helpless or depressed.

Some bad events really are uncontrollable, such as a tornado destroying your house. The explanation for why that happened to you and not someone else is just plain bad luck. Any further attempt at explaining such a disaster in more personal terms ("Because I'm a bad person and I deserved it," or "I knew I shouldn't have bought such an expensive summer house near the ocean") is an attempt to take more responsibility for uncontrollable events than is reasonable. Individuals who spend a lot of time second-guessing themselves in this manner are more prone to depression because they try to control everything, even those things that cannot possibly be controlled.

Most of life's events, however, are not quite so uncontrollable as having your house hit by a tornado. Reality is usually somewhat ambiguous. Let's take an example most people can identify with: You apply for a job that sounds exactly like what you are looking for. After what you think is a successful interview, you are told that you are one of three final candidates for the position. You are elated at the prospect of getting such a perfect position, but try to remain calm so you will not be too disappointed if you are not selected. One week later, you receive the bad news: you were not chosen for the job.

According to the revised learned helplessness theory, all of us have our own characteristic way of explaining bad events (such as not getting the job) when reality is ambiguous. The theory says that people explain an event as being caused by different combinations of something:

1. Stable versus unstable.
2. Global versus specific.
3. Internal versus external.

Let's look at each explanation using the job example.

1. *Stable:* If you explain not getting this job as something *stable* over time ("I never get the job that I really want"), you will expect it to happen again and show signs of helplessness in similar situations in the future.

   Unstable: If you explain it as something *unstable*

over time ("This was unusual. I usually get jobs that I'm qualified for and that I really want"), you will not expect a disappointment like this to happen again, and will not feel helpless in similar future situations.

2. *Global:* If you explain it in *global* terms ("I almost never achieve my goals. This is just one more example"), you will expect bad things to happen to you in all areas of your life, and continue to feel helpless.

   Specific: If you explain it in *specific* terms ("Well, I didn't get this job, but I've gotten others I wanted, and I'll try again for something else"), then you will feel hopeful about the future.

3. *Internal:* If you explain not getting the job as *internal* ("It was all my fault. I know that if I had done better in the interview, I might have gotten the job"), then you are likely to have lowered self-confidence and self-esteem in the future.

   External: If you explain not getting the job as *external* ("Well, I know I did the best I could. They must have found someone else whom they thought would do better in the job"), then your self-esteem and self-confidence remain intact in spite of the disappointment of not getting the job.

You are probably starting to catch on to the pattern here—it is not necessarily *what* happens to you that increases your stress and risk for depression, it is *how* you explain what happened. In the job example, reality is usually a combination of a little of all the factors: perhaps you might have done better in your interview, and that might have increased your chances of getting the job, but it is probably also true that they found another well-qualified person to take the job. While it is not healthy to take responsibility for everything, it is also not healthy to give up responsibility for everything and be a victim. Something in between is the healthiest response.

In evaluating your risk for depression, a person who tends to explain things in the following ways is at the highest risk for depression when bad events do occur:

- *Stable*—"It's this way and will always be this way."
- *Global*—"It's going to affect everything that I do."
- *Internal*—"It's all my fault."

All of these five factors are environmental, or psychosocial, factors that place an individual at higher risk for depression. If they apply to you, don't despair. They are external factors that can be changed. Once you are aware of the problems you can work on changing your attitudes or finding better social support and minimizing stressful life events. In chapter 4, which focuses on prevention, we will discuss the many ways in which you can minimize the risk factors that are strongest in your particular situation.

Who Is at Risk for Depression: The Demographics

While depression is a nondiscriminating illness that affects people of all ages, races, genders, and socioeconomic classes, demographic statistics indicate that the rate of depression is higher in some categories than in others. Age, gender, marital status, social class, education, race, occupation, and other factors may affect the risk for depression. Let's look at each individually:

Age

Before the 1940s, depression was perceived as an illness that primarily affected the middle-aged and the elderly. The typical depressed individual was a person in the forty- to sixty-year-old range. Before World War II, statistics compiled by the National Institute of Mental Health (NIMH) showed that the average age of first onset of depressive symptoms was forty. More recent statistics indicate that the average age of onset is now much lower, in the mid-twenties. In fact, depression now occurs most often among the "baby-boomers," those individuals who are between twenty-five and forty-five years old. Ironically, the stereotype of the depressed older person in his or her fifties or sixties is no longer accurate—a recent study found that senior citizens who are sixty and over are the least depressed of any age group.

Why has the age for first onset of depression dropped so much in the last forty years? Why is it so prevalent among the twenty-five- to forty-five-year-old group, an age when individuals should be in the prime of their lives?

Some researchers have dubbed the 1970s and 1980s the "Age of Melancholy" because of the increase in depression in the past two decades. One explanation suggests that the 1940s, 1950s, and 1960s made up the "Age of Anxiety," a period when mankind's development and use of nuclear weapons gave us the power to destroy our entire species. Along with this awareness came the anxiety, the worries. However, as we moved through the 1960s into the 1970s and 1980s, there was much speculation that the dominant mood was shifting from anxiety to depression and despair. This Age of Melancholy may have developed because the rising expectations for greater world cooperation and peace that reached crescendos at the end of World War II and again during the social revolution of the 1960s were dashed.

One psychological theory holds that depression results when there is a large gap between expectation and reality. Individuals feel depressed not so much because a situation is bad, but because they had expected better. The resulting disappointment and giving up of hope are the seeds of depression and despair.

Does this theory explain why the rates of depression have increased and why the age of onset is so much lower? Taken alone, perhaps not, but as one of several explanations, including the theory that rates of depression have increased because the illness is better diagnosed, it is certainly plausible.

The theory helps to explain only the increased *tendency* toward depression in the past two decades because depression, even at highest estimates, affects only 25 percent of the total population.

Gender

Much like the increased rate of depression among younger individuals, the rate of depression among women has increased greatly over the past forty years.

Estimates show that women are two to three times more likely to be diagnosed with depressive illness than are men. One out of every four women will suffer from major depression in her lifetime, compared to only one out of every ten men. Experts suggest that if cases of mild, undiagnosed depression were considered, the odds that a woman will suffer from symptoms of depression would be even higher.

While there may not yet be agreement on what causes the higher rate of depression, there is agreement that women are at higher risk for depression than are men. Many explanations have been suggested, including social discrimination, the unfulfilled expectations of the women's liberation movement, and hormonal factors as well as the fact that women are more likely to seek professional help and report feelings of depression. (In chapter 7, you will find an in-depth discussion of the increased risk of depression among women.) Other recent research points out the fact that economic and social pressures, combined with an increased willingness on the part of men to admit and discuss their emotional problems, may be increasing the rate of reported depression in men. But even with this increase, Dr. Myrna M. Weissman, professor of epidemiology in psychiatry at Columbia University and Dr. Gerald L. Klerman, professor of psychiatry at Cornell University Medical Center, quoted in a December 18, 1991, *New York Times* article, report that women are about twice as prone to depression as men are.

Even though women are at higher risk of suffering from depressive illness, men are at higher risk for the gravest consequence—suicide. According to NIMH statistics, victims of depression account for at least 60 percent of all suicides. An estimated 15 percent of clinically depressed persons commit suicide, as do approximately 25 percent of untreated manic depressives. The U.S. Centers for Disease Control (CDC) reports that there are almost 30,000 reported suicides each year. (The actual number is probably higher, since many "accidents" may actually have been unreported suicides.) Men attempt—and succeed—at committing suicide two to three times more often than do women. In the age group of men between fifteen and thirty-four years, suicide is the third leading cause of death (after accidents and homicides).

Marital Status

At first glance, one might guess that being married would be a positive factor—a hedge against depression—because of the security, companionship, and social support (indeed, a confidant) that it offers. And being married does decrease the risk for depression among men. Statistics show that married men are less depressed than are single, divorced, or widowed men. (Among men, those who are widowers have the highest rate of depression.) So for men, marriage seems to be a positive factor.

For women, though, marriage may be a slightly different story. Research has indicated that the mental health of married women is worse than that of single women and married men. Married women have a higher rate of depression than do single and divorced women, and a similar rate of depression when compared to widows. Why would marriage be hazardous to a woman's mental health? Once again, there are many explanations, including the pressures of being a mother and wife, of giving up a career in favor of child rearing, and the necessity of making adjustments to marriage.

A word of caution here: This is not to imply that all married women are depressed or at risk for depression. There are certainly many women who are happily married. Statistics are generalizations and indicate trends for an entire group, not for individuals. As a *group*, married women have higher rates of depression than do nonmarried women.

Social Class

Depression is found among all socioeconomic classes, from the homeless to the very wealthy. Not surprisingly, the rates of depression are slightly higher among the lower socioeconomic classes. Poverty, contributing to the inability to have control over one's life, could increase the risk for both major and mild depression.

The only exception to this is manic-depressive illness. Manic-depression is one of the few mental disorders that shows a higher prevalence in upper socioeconomic groups. It is also almost as prevalent among men as among women. Why is this so? Researchers really do not know why, but they speculate that it may have to do with the strong biochemical (and thus genetic) basis of manic-depression. Such a strong biological basis would negate the effects of environmental factors such as poverty, as well. It might also be more prevalent among men than depression is because social discrimination and socialization factors would not play as strong a role in manic-depression as they might in other types of depression, since it is acceptable for men to be very active.

Education

Statistical evidence is inconclusive on whether the level of education affects an individual's risk for depression. Some studies indicate that people who have college or graduate degrees have higher rates of depression than those who have never attended college. However, other studies have demonstrated just the opposite—that people who have only a high school education have a greater incidence of depression than do college-educated individuals. It seems that education is less of a factor than is the nature of one's work or occupation.

Race

In the United States, individuals who are "people of color" (or racial/ethnic minorities), such as blacks, Asians, Indians, and Hispanics, are at a slightly higher risk for depression than are whites. Studies in this area have focused upon black versus white rates of depression, while attempting to control confounding factors such as socioeconomic class and education. When black individuals were matched with white individuals who were as similar as possible in regard to education, class, occupation, location of residence, etc., the black group had a higher incidence of depression than did the white group. Sociologists explain the increased prevalence of depression in ethnic minority groups by citing the negative effects of racial discrimination in the United States.

Occupation

Demographic statistics have shown that some occupations have a higher rate of stress-related problems, such as alcoholism, drug abuse, and suicide. Those who hold occupations that are high in stress, including police officers, doctors, dentists, air traffic controllers, managers, and anyone who is responsible for other people's lives, are at a higher risk for depression than those in occupations that are lower in stress. This certainly does not mean that individuals working in occupations that are lower in stress do not suffer from depression. Low-stress positions often are high in boredom, which may lead to depression in some individuals. And other individuals thrive in high-stress positions. Like other environmental factors, occupational stress is a generalized factor reflecting group, not individual, tendencies.

What do all of these environmental factors mean in your personal case? If you have several of the environmental factors associated with high risk, then your chances of being depressed are increased.

How does this work? Let's look at our example of Susan again. We already know that she has an increased risk of inheriting the predisposition for depression because of her family history. What are her environmental risks in addition to her genetic risk?

First, Susan's mother had a history of depression as Susan was growing up. It is very likely that she "learned" some of the behaviors exhibited by her mother. These behaviors may include withdrawing into one's own world (refusing to leave one's room or house, for instance) when under stress and avoiding difficulties.

Having watched her mother's helplessness in coping with depression, Susan may have intuitively or subconsciously learned some of the same behaviors—behaviors that become apparent when she is under stress herself as an adult.

In further interviews, we learned that Susan has experienced several stressful life events in the past twelve months. She and her husband, Tim, recently moved from Los Angeles to Boston because of a new job for her husband. In addition to all the changes in location of home, job, etc., Susan has lost her confidante, a friend who still lives in California. Not having a support system is a big loss for Susan because of the increased stress of living in a new location.

What about Susan's attitudes? Do they put her at higher risk for depression? When asked about the ways in which she explained events that happened to her, Susan's replies fell into the *unstable, global,* and *internal* categories. Her attitude toward bad events is *unstable* because she feels she is usually able to handle difficult situations: "I think that I can usually make friends; I just haven't had the opportunity yet." (This attitude is positive because it puts her at a lesser risk for depression.)

However, Susan's attitude toward bad events does tend to be *global.* She is beginning to expect bad things to happen to her in many areas of her life: "Nothing seems to go right for me. I had just gotten settled in one job and then we moved. I feel helpless about controlling my life sometimes." (This attitude is a negative one and puts her at a greater risk for depression.)

More recently, Susan has started to have an *internal*

outlook on events. She feels that she is responsible for bad events even when they are not her fault: "If I had gotten a different degree I wouldn't be stuck in the job situation I am. I should work harder at making my marriage work. If we fight, it's usually my fault because I think I'm taking my unhappiness out on Tim." This internal attitude is negative because it focuses blame on herself when it has not necessarily been in her control to do anything about the situation.

Given Susan's attitudinal style, recent stressful life events, family history, and loss of a support system, it is no surprise that she is beginning to exhibit signs of depression. She is at high risk because of environmental factors. Yet she is not helpless or powerless. There are many ways that Susan can prevent her depression from getting any worse. She can also treat many of the early symptoms now.

If you find that you have some of the environmental risks for depression, you, like Susan, can do something about it. Prevention is something that can definitely change your risk for depression (See chapter 4).

A New Theory of Environmental Risks: Is Depression Linked to the Seasons?

For years, people have been complaining that the reason that they are depressed is the long, dreary fall and winter. They report feeling much more lethargic and sleepy between October and March, sometimes gorging themselves on carbohydrates and gaining "winter weight." During the fall and winter, these individuals lose interest in sex, feel irritable, and have trouble concentrating on their work. In more extreme cases, they have many of the symptoms of major depression—some even to the point where they consider suicide. There's one difference, though. When spring and summer return with their sunny, balmy days, they recover quickly, almost miraculously. They become happy, productive, optimistic individuals. That is, until the fall and winter seasons blow in again, and their cycle of depression repeats.

Up until a decade ago, professionals and researchers thought that this seasonal link to depression was either in people's heads or was a coincidence. Now there is new evidence that some individuals do suffer from a depression known as *SAD*, an acronym for *seasonal affective disorder*. People who have symptoms of SAD grow increasingly depressed as the summer wanes and the days become shorter and shorter in the fall and winter.

Scientists now believe that SAD is triggered by the decreased amount of sunlight these individuals experience in the winter. Since it is known that the amount of light affects behavior in animals in different ways, including determining reproductive cycles, researchers thought that the amount of light might affect human behavior as well.

The scientists' work has focused upon the pineal gland, a tiny gland at the base of the brain that secretes melatonin. Melatonin is a hormone that plays an important role in maintaining the biological clock that keeps our body rhythms on their daily cycles. Mela-

tonin also makes humans feel lethargic, tired, and
drained. Researchers have now found that light sup-
presses the production of melatonin. As the theory goes,
the decreased amount of natural light in the fall and
winter seasons increases the amount of melatonin secreted during the darker, colder months, and individuals feel more lethargic, sleepy, and perhaps more
depressed and hopeless.

Why was SAD not known before 1980 and why has
it come to attention at this time? Scientists have just
begun to understand the effects of light upon melatonin
production. In the past, people used to be exposed to
more sunlight, even in the winter, but with the advent
of windowless or darker office buildings, factories, and
shopping malls, modern workers might spend all day
without any exposure to natural sunlight.

The profile of the typical individual suffering from
SAD is a woman (there are three to four times as many
female SAD sufferers as males) in her early thirties who
has had these symptoms for years. She has always felt
depressed in the winter, energetic and cheerful in the
summer, but has never understood *why* the seasons
have such control over her mood.

Let's look at an example. Peg, thirty-four, a mother
of two young children, is an accountant who lives in
Maine, where the winters are long and usually cloudy.
Ever since she was in high school, she remembers going
into a slump in October, feeling more hopeless and depressed through the winter. She reports,

> I hated the Christmas season. I remember hiding up
> in my room, pretending to have a stomachache so I
> wouldn't have to come downstairs and pretend to be

cheerful. As I got older I had to keep functioning, even in the dark of winter, but it was very hard. Getting out of bed was a major effort, and some days I had to return home after noon because I felt so weepy and depressed. It had gotten so bad that I went to see several doctors, two of whom gave me antidepressant medication, but nothing seemed to work. But in the warm spring and summer months I was an entirely different person. I felt so good that I worked all day and still had time for softball practice, Little League games, swimming, picnics, you name it. But when the leaves would start to drop in the autumn, so would my spirits. It got so bad that I began to look into moving to a warmer climate, like Florida or California, but because of my husband's job, we just couldn't move. I really felt stuck.

Luckily for Peg and others like her who suffer from symptoms of SAD, there seems to be some relief available now. The treatment for SAD is light therapy, which attempts to reproduce the light conditions of the summer through specially designed fluorescent lights that include all the colors found in natural sunlight, from far-red to ultraviolet, and produces 2,500 lux (one lux equals approximately the light of a candle per square meter of space). The standard fluorescent lighting in an office is only 500 lux, but the light outdoors at noon on a sunny summer day is about 110,000 lux. SAD sufferers sit in front of these special lights for three to four hours a day.

Researchers report that slight improvements in mood occur within three to four days of this light therapy treatment. Consistent treatment usually continues for at least a month, when SAD sufferers are put on lower maintenance dosages of these special lights for one to two hours a day. It is too early to say whether light therapy treatment works for all who exhibit SAD symptoms, but it seems to be effective for most, including Peg. She happily reports,

> I can't believe the difference it has made in my life. I have started to have almost as much energy in the winter months as I do in the summer. This Christmas, I was able to buy and decorate a tree, and even organize a holiday party. My children were so delighted. They have their mother back again, all twelve months of the year.

Unlike Peg, many individuals with SAD don't have symptoms of moderate to major depression in the fall and winter. Instead, some may suffer from mild symptoms of feeling tired, depressed, irritable, and lethargic in the winter, while functioning quite well in other seasons. These individuals, although not requiring intensive light therapy treatment, might feel their mood lift if they were exposed to more natural sunlight during the winter months, or were exposed to the special fluorescent lights for short periods of time.

But fall and winter are not the only seasons that seem to be a factor in depression. Some individuals become depressed during the summer, when the sun is at its hottest. In a reverse form of SAD, summer itself and/or the accompanying heat may be an environmental stress that can cause depression.

Studies have shown a high correlation between the

summer months and increases in the rates of aggressive behavior and violent crimes. Not only are there more assaults, rapes, and murders (some of which might be explained because more people are outdoors), but there is also an increase in crimes such as wife battering and other crimes that generally occur indoors.

While the phenomenon of "summer depression" is far less known and less widely studied than SAD, researchers have reported a number of cases in which individuals report being much more depressed in the summer months. Most attribute the depression to the heat.

One such case is that of Nancy, a forty-year-old journalist. For at least ten years, Nancy found that she felt very sad and had many symptoms of depression during the summer months, including frequent crying spells, feelings of inadequacy, an inability to perform her usual job responsibilities, and thoughts of suicide. When the heat and humidity lifted, Nancy generally felt better and more in control of herself. As fall came, she was able to return to work. Her life seemed to go along well until it became warm and sticky again in the month of May.

Then, Nancy could almost feel the gloom and depression returning. She could not bear to go through another depressing summer and consulted several doctors. One tried several antidepressant medications, but none of them had any effect. As a last resort, Nancy's doctor suggested that she try to remain in an extra-cool environment all of the time. So she stayed in an air-conditioned room with temperatures below 65 degrees Fahrenheit and took long cold showers several times a day for an entire week, at the end of which she reported that she began to feel much better. No longer feeling desperate or weepy, Nancy continued this cool environment and cold shower treatment for the entire summer. It turned out to be the most productive and enjoyable summer she had experienced in ten years.

Did Nancy suffer from summer depression? Scientists differ in how they conceptualize this problem. Some believe that there is such a phenomenon as summer depression that affects individuals only in the summer months, much as people with SAD have depressive symptoms only during the winter months. Other scientists are not convinced of a biochemical basis for summer depression. They feel that some people simply have trouble with the hot, sticky weather. These people become so uncomfortable in the heat that they have trouble sleeping, become irritable, and as a result, may have lowered energy and self-esteem, and may demonstrate symptoms of depression during the summer.

Whether or not there is such a thing as summer depression remains to be seen, but it is clear that summer can be a stressful time for some individuals who have more trouble coping with heat than others. For them, many of whom may already have a predisposition to depression, the stress of the heat may put them over the edge.

The research in this area suggests that climate, the amount of sunlight, humidity, temperature, and the seasons may affect human behavior and mental health more than we previously might have thought. Some people have always reported being more depressed during one season than another, but most doctors have considered it to be "all in their heads." Now the scientific evidence is beginning to show that it may, in fact, be all in their body chemistry.

While psychological reactions to environmental stresses differ from individual to individual, for those at risk for depression, these factors may tip the balance between seasons of well-being and seasons of depression.

4

Can Depression Be Prevented?

While the predisposition to depression, along with environmental factors, may make the potential for depression higher for some individuals, it does not make it inevitable. Depression can be prevented if appropriate precautionary measures are taken. But what works for one person may not necessarily work for another. Prevention programs should be individualized for each person depending upon specific symptoms, personality style, and goals.

What Are the Important Factors in Prevention?

First, you should make an inventory of the symptoms you may have but need to prevent. Depression can come in different forms. What form does depression take for you? Answer the questions in this Depression Inventory to determine your particular profile.

Depression Inventory

1. When you are depressed, do you:

   - Cry easily? _____
   - Have problems sleeping? _____
   - Have eating problems (either overeating or no appetite)? _____
   - Feel worthless? _____
   - Have a lack of energy? _____
   - Become irritable? _____
   - Feel like hurting yourself or ending it all? _____
   - Drink too much alcohol? _____
   - Lose interest in previously enjoyable activities?_____
   - Get angry easily? _____

2. How long does a typical depressive episode last? (Answer should be in days, weeks, or months.)_____

3. How many times do you recall having been depressed in the past ten years? _____

4. Are you depressed at specific times of the year, such as during winter or summer? _____

5. Are you depressed at specific times of the year in relation to specific events, such as anniversaries of births or deaths? _____

6. Are there specific times of the day or night when you tend to feel more depressed and immobilized? _____

7. Do you also have manic episodes during which you are full of energy and feel like you can accomplish anything?

_____

If yes, how long do these episodes usually last? _____

8. Are you taking any medication that could cause depression as a side effect? _____

9. When you are feeling depressed, do you feel better if you are active and doing something? _____

10. Do you have someone to whom you can turn when you start to feel depressed and unhappy? _____

By answering the questions to this Depression Inventory, you can develop your own profile and will be able to identify the steps that will help you to prevent the onset of symptoms of depression.

Let's look at Susan again. After filling out the Depression Inventory, this is the profile that she developed for herself:

When I am depressed, I:

- Cry easily, particularly if I am criticized.
- Have trouble sleeping at night, but am sleepy during the day.
- Have little appetite. Food is not appealing.
- Feel tired and have no energy.
- Want to stay in bed to avoid the world.
- Have little interest in anything.

I have experienced two episodes of what I would consider mild depression. I was able to get out of bed and get myself to work. I wasn't productive at all, though, and felt worthless. Each episode lasted about a month. When the depression improved, it happened slowly. I began to feel slightly better, more in control, and I woke up with more energy each day. It took about two weeks before I started to feel "normal" again.

I don't think there was any pattern in terms of when I became depressed. As I recall, the first time was two years ago in March and the most recent was three months ago, in June.

During the day, I felt discouraged and guilty, but it was really in the evening hours and at night that I felt the worst. A sense of despair and hopelessness would overtake me after nightfall. I desperately wanted to come home to my room but once I was there I would feel trapped. If I was somewhere other than at home, I was preoccupied with the desire to leave as soon as possible to return home.

As far as manic episodes go, I can't say that I have ever experienced one. I generally have a pretty high level of energy, but I would not consider it to be excessive.

I don't usually take medication of any sort, other than antibiotics if I am sick or aspirin for fever and pain now and then. I don't think that any of these medications cause depression.

When I feel depressed I realize that I would feel better if I could do something active. However, it is during those times of depression that I have the hardest times getting myself to *move*. I cannot motivate myself to do anything even though I know that if I went out, I would feel better.

When I start to feel unhappy and depressed, I become so irritable that it is hard for me to get support from anyone. No matter what anyone says, particularly my husband or a close friend, I get more defensive. Then I start to feel angry at them because they don't understand the pain I'm experiencing. Lots of times my husband says it's all in my head and I can make it go away by myself. He would never say that if he really understood the nature of what I was experiencing. So I just don't tell him or anyone else anymore. It's too frustrating.

As we can see from Susan's answers, she has an individual depression profile that is uniquely her own. She seems to have a good understanding of her symptoms and problems, and can learn to apply this knowledge in order to prevent further episodes of depression.

What Is Involved in Prevention of Depression?

One of the key factors in prevention of depression is changing the conditions under which you are depressed. In other words, make the conditions too difficult for depression to grab hold and to exist. In Susan's case, she could establish a confidant relationship, so she'll have someone to share problems and difficulties with. Susan has already stated that she is unable to use her husband or any close friends as confidants. Developing a confidant relationship takes time, and perhaps luck, but Susan does not have the time to wait for this relationship to happen.

While it would be ideal for Susan to have a true confidant, the most efficient thing for her to do in the meantime is to find a psychotherapist. Ideally, this therapist should be someone in whom she has confidence and whom she can trust to give her support and sound advice. Additionally, her psychotherapist should be someone who can challenge her to change old patterns. It would be desirable, although not essential, for her psychotherapist to have some experience treating adults with depression. Psychotherapy should provide a place where she can discuss unashamedly her feelings of worthlessness, sensitivity to criticism, and despair. The psychotherapist, whether a psychologist, psychiatrist, or social worker, should be able to help Susan to cope with these strong, negative emotions.

The ability to be objective, challenging, and yet supportive is something that even a well-meaning friend or relative frequently may not have. Sometimes it is necessary to find a professional who can listen to negative feelings, give helpful, objective feedback, and work with you toward a plan to avoid the depression.

If you have a relationship with a confidant in which you feel comfortable discussing feelings and problems, you are fortunate. Being able to discuss problems as soon as they occur will help you to cope with stressful events. But if you don't have such a relationship, and even if you do but could use more feedback and support, you should consider working with a psychotherapist *before* you become depressed.

Preventing depression if you are vulnerable to the illness requires that you work actively at making your own living situation as positive as possible. Creating a positive living situation means focusing on optimizing conditions to fight depression. For some individuals this might include development of a support system (a sort of "safety net" if things go wrong), keeping active and physically fit, and getting professional help when things look stressful. For others, it might mean slowing down the pace, being more relaxed, or doing meditation. The bottom line for everyone is the same. Do things in your life that help to raise your self-esteem and make you feel good about yourself. By taking control of your life situation, you will be less likely to feel helpless and depressed. Let's look at Susan's example again.

Susan knows that she is one of those people who is less likely to feel depressed if she keeps active. She reported that she becomes more depressed during the evening hours than during the day. Susan knows that she needs to be more active in the evening but has difficulty initiating anything. She is someone who would benefit from structured activities such as aerobic exercise classes, exercise and running clubs, swimming lessons, etc. Unless the activity is structured as a class or Susan has a friend or buddy who will make sure that they go swimming or biking or running together, Susan cannot depend on herself to do something in the evening hours after work. The activity should be started and maintained before she feels depressed, because once she starts to feel depressed, she will be unable to find and sustain an activity. Prevention requires anticipating what you need before you need it.

Psychological research conducted by John H. Greist, coauthor of *Depression and Its Treatment: Help for the Nation's #1 Mental Problem* (American Psychiatric Press, 1984), has shown that being active is an effective way of avoiding depression and mental illness. Researchers examining the effects of exercise have found a strong correlation between physical fitness and mental health, with some studies showing that exercising for half an hour a day can improve both physical fitness and the mental outlook of an individual. Because of the beneficial aspects of physical fitness, some clinicians prescribe exercise programs as a means of treating symptoms of depression and anxiety.

As a preventive measure, Susan should be involved in an exercise regimen on a daily basis. This exercise could take the form of whatever activity she enjoys the most, whether it be jogging, swimming, bicycling, aerobic classes, brisk walking, or tennis. While other sports are also helpful, aerobic exercise, such as swimming, biking, or any form of exercise that gets the heart rate up to 80 percent of its maximum potential, for at least 20 minutes, is the most beneficial.

The Role of Aerobic Exercise

Why is aerobic exercise so helpful in fighting depression? It is effective because consistent exercisers seem to receive both psychological and physiological benefits. The psychological benefits of exercise include:

- Improvement of self-esteem and self-confidence.
- Elevation of mood.
- Feeling of relaxation.
- Feeling of control of one's body.
- Improved body image and self-image.
- Help in coping with stress and tension.

These benefits have been consistently reported by individuals who perform aerobic exercise on a regular basis, generally three to four days a week for at least 30 minutes a day. The psychological reinforcement of physical exercise is so strong that many consistent exercisers are considered to be "addicted to exercise." This addiction is generally perceived to be a positive one, as exercisers become dependent upon the many benefits of a regular regimen of aerobic exercise.

As for the physiological, or biochemical, benefits from consistent aerobic activity, it has been suggested that running and other strenuous aerobic exercise produce specific biochemical effects that may, at least in part, account for the positive psychological benefits and the "runner's high" described by athletes. This is a pleasurable feeling of relaxation and euphoria sometimes experienced after at least an hour of exercising.

The substances suspected of producing these feelings of exercise-induced euphoria (a state of mind incompatible with depression) are called endorphins, the body's self-produced natural painkillers. These compounds affect the parts of the brain that process information about pain, emotion, and feelings. Beta-endorphins (the name for the most commonly occurring type of endorphin in the body), when injected into the brain intravenously, tend to cause analgesia, a state of insensitivity to pain without loss of consciousness. Several research studies have demonstrated an increase in the levels of endorphins in the bloodstream after running and other strenuous exercise. This increase in endorphin levels indicates that the production and release into the body of endorphins during exercise may explain the pleasurable feelings of the "runner's high" and the sense of relaxation that often accompanies strenuous exercise.

In addition, it has been discovered that the production of these endorphins is low in depressed persons. The ability to increase endorphin production through exercise would be a major benefit to individuals who are depressed or who are vulnerable to depression. This area of research is new and scientists are not yet certain how endorphins are produced during strenuous exercise. However, the physiological and psychological benefits of exercise for those who are vulnerable to depression are widely accepted.

So get moving! If you are not physically active, you should develop an exercise program that will allow you to gradually increase the amount of exercise you do, so that you're *aerobically active* at least three times a week for a minimum of 20 minutes per session. There are many adult physical education classes that you could join. Aerobic classes are popular, particularly among women, or if you prefer to work out independently, very brisk walking, jogging, swimming, and bicycling can all be fun and beneficial.

Some people report that they are too tired or have no time for exercise. You will find that although you might feel physically exhausted for a short time after exercise, you will likely feel mentally energized and awake. Many people report that their minds are much more alert and they feel better in general after exercising. Finding time to exercise can seem difficult, but you can also be creative and efficient in finding ways to get "double benefits" from exercise. You can walk, run, or bike part of your way to work. One woman who drives to work now regularly parks her car one mile from her workplace, briskly walking the mile to and from work. Other people swim, walk, or exercise during their lunch hours. Even mothers can take their young children on long stroller rides and complete a long brisk walk while doing errands. Exercise has been shown to be effective in preventing depression and treating symptoms of depression, but to be effective, it has to be done on a consistent basis. Make the commitment and you'll see the change.

Other Techniques for Preventing Depression

Doctors and clinicians who work with depressed people report that the most common reason for people getting depressed and remaining depressed is that they become stuck in a negative frame of mind that they are unable to change. As I have said to clients, negative things—even minor events—happen, and everything starts to mushroom. Soon, it is easy to become discouraged and frustrated. After a few failed attempts to solve problems, people start to feel depressed about everything, even things they can do something about. It's all too easy to get stuck in a rut of negative thinking—and all too hard to change one's thinking around and get back on track.

The best treatment for depression is not to get depressed in the first place. In addition to the other prevention techniques already mentioned, you can work at preventing depression through developing a positive frame of mind.

What does it mean to have a positive frame of mind? The concept of developing a positive frame of mind is based upon the *cognitive theory of depression*, one of the three major psychological theories to explain depression and treatment of depression.

Cognitive theory was first introduced by Dr. Aaron Beck in the 1960s. It is based on the premise that cognition, or how you are thinking about things, your perspective, your view of life, controls your feelings and moods. Cognition includes your mental attitudes, your beliefs, and the way that you interpret your life experiences.

The main principle of cognitive theory focuses on the role that thought processes play in the way we feel. Beck theorized that when individuals feel depressed, their thoughts are dominated by a pervasive negativity. These people perceive themselves and the world in negative, distorted ways. They look back on their past and remember all the unpleasant, unhappy things. They dwell on the negative aspects of their current lives. Worse of all, they visualize their future and cannot imagine anything other than problems, despair, and unhappiness.

Cognitive theorists believe that the negative thoughts that form the foundation of depressed people's emotional turmoil almost always contain gross distortions. So, although the negative thoughts may be based on reality or fact, reality is distorted in a way that is irrational. With enough distortion, depressed people soon believe that things really are as bad as they thought, and this distorted thinking becomes one of the causes of their depression.

Thus, cognitive theory explains depression by saying that depression is not based on accurate perceptions of reality, but is really the product of inaccurate, distorted thinking. Distorted thinking becomes a part of a vicious cycle that is hard to get out of.

How does this relate to you and your feelings of depression? Let's take another example. Barbara, a young woman about to graduate from law school, is usually a pleasant, well-adjusted woman who has her ups and downs. However, when she feels down, she perceives things differently, actually feels differently than when she is not depressed. Her thoughts are filled with negativity. She becomes preoccupied with all the unhappiness she has experienced in the past. Recently, when she broke up with her steady boyfriend, Barbara relived in her mind all the sad breakups she had experienced since she was a teenager. "Nobody ever likes me enough to stay with me," she thought. "I'll never find anyone who will love me once he finds out how worthless I really am. In the beginning of a relationship, people might find me attractive but once they discover what a loser I am, they will leave me too."

Barbara is not such a loser, but when she feels depressed, she convinces herself that she is inadequate and unworthy of love. When she is not feeling upset, she has a positive image of herself, and is quite successful at most things that she attempts. However, when she is upset, her negative thoughts take over her thinking. These negative thoughts, which are distortions and not reality, become the actual cause of her emotions of unhappiness and despair. Most people think that their negative thoughts are the symptoms of their depression, but cognitive theorists believe that negative thoughts are both a symptom and a cause of depression.

Dr. David Burns is a cognitive theorist who developed a list of cognitive distortions to explain how depression develops as a result of negative thinking. In his book, *Feeling Good: The New Mood Therapy* (William Morrow, 1980), he lists these cognitive distortions:

1. *All-or-nothing thinking:* This refers to the tendency to evaluate things in extreme terms. Unless you are perfect and do everything correctly, you will see any failure as proof that you are inadequate or worthless. For example, a competitive runner who has won many marathons in the past has a bad day and cannot finish the Boston marathon. Instead of balancing this loss with his many wins, he thinks, "They say that you are only as good as your last race. I'm sure that everyone will forget about me as a runner and I'll never get any sponsorships again. I always thought some of my wins were flukes; now everyone else will know." Of course, the runner is exaggerating the effect of one poor showing, but if he starts to believe it himself, he will become depressed enough to start the vicious circle of self-doubt and depression. None of us is perfect; we all make mistakes and fail at times. If we distort our reality with all-or-nothing thinking we will be constantly depressed because our expectations will never conform to reality.

2. *Overgeneralization:* This refers to the ways in which we make our slight disappointments into something much bigger. Most of the times when we feel rejected we are guilty of overgeneralizing. For example, a student gathers up her courage to try out for a play. She is hopeful of getting a small part. When the casting list is posted and she is not on it, she feels extremely disappointed. To feel dis-

appointed is common, but then she begins to over-generalize this one failure. She thinks to herself, "I'll never become an actress. Not only that, but all of my friends will see that I'm untalented and they won't want to associate with me. How will I face my parents? They'll realize that they wasted all their money sending me to college." In her distorted way of thinking, this aspiring young actress has concluded that because she was not selected for one play, her friends and family will not find her to be a worthy person. She has overgeneralized one rejection into a massive rejection of herself by others.

3. *Mental filter:* When you are depressed, you do the opposite of "looking at the world through rose-colored glasses." Instead, you have a pair of eyeglasses that filters out any positive experiences. You allow only negative thoughts to fill your mind. For example, a depressed man suffered a negative experience. He found a parking space on a busy street. As he was getting ready to back into the space, a small car zoomed in and took it. The man told the small car's driver that he had been waiting for the space and was there first, but the driver said, "Too bad. *My* car's in the space now." The depressed man became enraged at the driver's selfishness. The unfairness of the situation made him feel angry but helpless. He decided that the world was full of nasty, selfish people. What he did not consider was that this was an isolated incident and that over the past few months, few, if any, people had behaved as unfairly as did the

driver of the small car. In fact, there were several instances in which strangers had been particularly helpful to him, but he did not think about any of the positive experiences. His mental filter was working to filter out any positive experiences and focus only on the negative ones.

4. *Disqualifying the positive:* Another common technique that depressed people use is to transform positive statements and experiences into negative ones. For example, when someone compliments your work, you say, "Oh, it was nothing. Everyone did well on the exam. It was easy." You are mentally disqualifying the compliment, and after a while, you start to believe that it was nothing yourself. Individuals who use this form of cognitive distortion lack self-confidence and self-esteem. They usually believe that there is something inadequate about themselves and their work. They live in fear that someone will catch on to what they fear (even though it isn't true)—that they are inferior and that they have fooled everyone until now. Individuals who disqualify the positive put things out of balance: they dwell on negative experiences and assign more importance to failures while downplaying successes and positive experiences.

5. *Jumping to conclusions:* People who are depressed frequently make the mistake of concluding something negative without gathering all the information. For example, you walk into your office in the morning. Two of your co-workers are talking excitedly to each other. When you get near them, hope-

ful to join in the conversation, they stop talking, smile, say hello, and return to their offices. You immediately conclude that you are being excluded, that they don't like you, or worse yet, that they were saying something negative about you. The reality could well be that the co-workers were talking about a mutual friend they have whom you do not know, and the reason they stopped talking was not because they dislike you, but because they realized it was time to start working when they saw you enter. Or they thought you would think badly of them for chatting on office time. Instead of these reasonably likely scenarios occurring to you, you dwell on the fact that you were excluded. These imagined rejections may cause you to be unfriendly to your co-workers the next time you see them. By jumping to conclusions, you have created a situation that becomes a self-fulfilling prophecy: you think they don't like you—you act in an unfriendly manner to them—they respond in an unfriendly way—and you are convinced you were right all along: they were talking about you and they don't like you! Making incorrect conclusions based on a small amount of evidence is a cognitive distortion that is very common among people who are depressed. Even when you find out that your worst fears were untrue, you may have unnecessarily spent a great deal of time feeling bad or miserable. Wait until you have more accurate information before jumping to negative conclusions.

6. *Emotional reasoning:* This refers to the way that many people accept their emotions as truths. This

kind of reasoning can be misleading because your feelings can actually reflect your thoughts and beliefs, not the other way around. For example, if you feel inadequate, you start to believe that you are a failure, or you may think, "I feel very overwhelmed; therefore my situation must be worse than I thought and impossible to improve. I may as well give up." For depressed people, emotional reasoning can be a strong roadblock to accomplishing anything. Because things can feel so negative and bad, you begin to believe that they really are that bad. Another example is the student who has to write a term paper. She thinks to herself, "The paper is so long and I feel so inadequately prepared to write it. It's hopeless." As the deadline to hand it in approaches she forces herself to begin the paper. Once she starts it, she realizes it is not that bad and she completes it on time. This is an example of how emotional reasoning can cause your negative feelings to delay your actions.

7. *Should statements:* Depressed people frequently feel a great deal of guilt and pressure, resulting in feelings of, "I *should* be a nicer person, or I *must* eat less." When you feel so much pressure and guilt, even if it is self-imposed, you start to feel resentful. Instead of doing the things you feel you should do, you rebel and do either the opposite or nothing at all. When the "shoulds" are imposed upon other people, you may feel let down because their actions don't meet your unrealistic expectations. People who have strong *should* demands are often unhappy because of the unmet, unrealistic

expectations placed upon themselves and others.

8. *Labeling and mislabeling:* Personal labeling is an extreme form of overgeneralization. Individuals who use this form of cognitive distortion label themselves "a failure" or "a bad mother," for example, because of one mistake or failing. When you say or feel, "I'm no good. I always fail at getting jobs," because you did not get a particular job, you are labeling and mislabeling yourself. Since your self, or who you are, cannot be equated with any one thing you do, labeling yourself because of your mistakes is a self-defeating and irrational thing to do. In reality, rather than being a constant entity, you are an ever-changing person who is sometimes successful, sometimes not. Labeling and mislabeling also is dangerous when we use it on other people. When you label other people, you usually distort their actions and see them only in light of the label you have given them. For example, a man who labels his mother-in-law a meddler will begin to see her every action as interfering with his life, and will jump on her inquiries about his family every chance he has. For the mother-in-law, if she labels the man an irresponsible slob, she will interpret every action of his to be that of a man trying to avoid fulfilling his responsibilities. In doing so, both of them will focus irrationally and unfairly on every mistake or imperfection as proof of the other person's worthlessness.

9. *Personalization:* This is a cognitive distortion that frequently results in guilt. It happens when you

take responsibility for something, usually a negative event, when there is no basis in reality for doing so. Even when you have done your part and you are not responsible for the outcome, you conclude that the failure is your fault or that it reflects your inadequacy. For example, let's assume that you organize a fund-raising event for an organization. You fulfill all of your duties, but only ten people show up to your event and it loses money. You conclude, "I am a poor organizer. It is my fault that the event lost money." Another example is a common one: When parents find out that their son is being suspended from school for fighting with other children, they conclude, "We must have been bad parents. I guess we have failed to raise our son to be a good boy."

While it is true that we all have some influence over other people, we do not have control over them, nor are we able to predict accurately how many participants an event will draw. Ultimately, what another person does is his or her responsibility, not yours, and you need to have a realistic sense of what you can and cannot do.

These nine cognitive distortions are common errors in thinking and perception that cause and help to perpetuate many depressive states. If you can understand how they work, and how they can be changed, you can actively prevent depression before it becomes so strong that you are helpless to do something about it.

Look carefully at your own perceptions and see if you use any of the cognitive distortions that have been described. When you find yourself feeling depressed, take an inventory of any ways you might be distorting reality and events. Take the time to do a "reality check" with someone you trust, either a confidant, a therapist or a close friend. Find out if your perceptions are correct. If they are, then you can work to change a negative situation into a positive one. If they are incorrect and distorted, then get help from a psychotherapist to correct your perceptions and the way they make you feel about yourself. Don't let cognitive distortions become a symptom *and* a cause of depression. Break the cycle early.

Let's look back at your depression profile. If you reported that you have many symptoms of depression, including thoughts of suicide, feelings of hopelessness, and manic episodes, you may need more help than a friend or confidant can provide. You should consider getting professional help now, before your depression gets worse. Many symptoms of depression can be treated through medication and other effective therapies, but you have to be diagnosed before you can be treated. And you have to take the first, sometimes painful, step of admitting that you are depressed and need help to work things out. In the next chapter you will find out what the differences are among mild, clinical, and severe depression, and how you can tell the difference in yourself and others.

5

Identifying the Symptoms and Understanding the Classifications of Depression

In chapter 1, the Depression Self-Test helped you to measure the severity of your depression. A list of symptoms of depression was included. You probably have a sense of where you fit in on the depression spectrum (from very mild depression to severe clinical depression). Yet, if you went to see a physician or therapist about your depression, he or she might use a number of different kinds of medical, psychological, or technical terms to describe your symptoms and your diagnosis. Since these terms may be unknown or unfamiliar to you, they will be explained in this chapter; once you understand what the professionals are talking about, you can then become an informed consumer or a patient actively participating in recovery.

The "Official" Definition of Depression

Depression, also known as depressive disorders, is defined as a spectrum of psychological and biological illnesses that vary in their severity, frequency, and duration. At one end of the spectrum is what is considered "normal, everyday" depression—a transient period of sadness and fatigue, usually developed as a response to clearly identifiable stressors, including any serious loss, disappointment, disaster, catastrophe, illness, or end of a relationship or marriage. The moods and symptoms associated with normal depression vary in length, but the general rule is that they continue no more than a period of two weeks. If the depressed mood and symptoms persist for a longer period of time, and more severe symptoms such as eating and sleeping difficulties, or feelings of hopelessness and despair develop, then the problem is considered to be a more serious depressive disorder.

On the more severe end of the spectrum are a number of disorders, including "psychotic depression." Individuals with psychotic depression not only suffer from the more serious symptoms of extreme sadness and hopelessness, but also may lose contact with reality, often experiencing delusions and hallucinations, and sometimes suffering severe motor and psychological retardation. (That is, they are so severely depressed that they can barely move or react appropriately.)

Since the term *depression* has been used, often indiscriminately, for the entire spectrum of depressive experiences and symptoms, it has been difficult to accurately measure and study the effects of depressive disorders. As a result, depression has been, and continues to be, considered a disease, a mood, a series of symptoms, and also a syndrome (a constellation of symptoms).

To make matters even more confusing, depressive disorders, unlike many other medical and psychological disorders, do not necessarily follow a predictable pattern of symptoms. Instead, they generally involve an unpredictable pattern of symptoms—some of which have been discussed earlier—including:

- Depressed mood—defined as sadness, despair, misery, gloom.
- Low self-esteem—loss of self-confidence and feelings of worth.
- General fatigue—lethargy, apathy.
- Guilt feelings—feelings of regret, self-blame.
- Appetite impairments—loss of interest in food or overeating.
- Sexual impairments—impotence, lack of interest in sex, infrequent sexual desire, promiscuity.
- Sleep impairments—insomnia and/or frequent awakenings, early awakening, or sleeping too much.
- Anger and irritability—negative attitudes, irritability.
- Delusions and hallucinations—losing touch with

reality, acting in a bizarre manner (occurs in more severe cases).

- Psychomotor agitation or retardation—speeding up or slowing down of physical activity.

Since the pattern of symptoms is so diverse and unpredictable (often covering two extremes of behavior such as insomnia and increased sleep, undereating and overeating), it has been hard to accurately diagnose and measure depression. Even still, several competing systems of classification have been developed in an attempt to define depression.

The oldest and currently the least popular system, the unitary system, assumes that there is only one type of depressive disorder, which varies in intensity. The mental health field generally dismisses this system, opting for a belief that there is more than one type of depressive disorder.

A more popular system of classification, the dualistic system, assumes that there are basically two groups of depressive disorders that complement or oppose each other. You may have heard of some of the names assigned to these dualistic types of depression. They include:

Group A	Group B
Reactive (depression in reaction to a stressful life event)	**Autonomous** (developing independently, or on its own)

Neurotic (relatively mild mental or emotional disorder, usually involving anxiety)

Psychotic (severe mental disorder with deterioration of functioning and partial or complete withdrawal from reality)

Exogenous (depression developed from external causes)

Endogenous (developed from within, originating within oneself)

In general, dualistic types of depression are based on distinctions between:

Group A factors	Group B factors
Less severe	More severe
Precipitated by life experiences	Unknown precipitation of symptoms, seemingly unrelated to life events
Short-term and relatively benign courses of depression	Long-term courses of depression and poor prognoses
Occurs only once or twice	High recurrence rate

There are also two other well-known dualistic conceptions of depression. The first is *primary versus secondary*. A diagnosis of "primary" disorder assumes that all the symptoms are attributable to depression; "secondary" refers to depression as a result of medical illnesses or other psychiatric illnesses. The division is usually based on two criteria:

1. When the depressive symptoms occurred in relation to an individual's medical and psychiatric history.
2. The presence or absence of associated illnesses.

Primary depression is diagnosed when the depression is unrelated to other psychiatric or medical illness. It is diagnosed in individuals who have previously been well or whose only previous psychiatric problem was manic-depressive illness or depression.

Secondary depression is diagnosed when depression is unrelated to any genetic predisposition and is a response to psychiatric illness, medical illness, surgery, or certain drugs. Some of the common psychiatric causes of secondary depression include schizophrenia and alcoholism. There are a number of possible physical causes of secondary depression including endocrine disorders associated with the thyroid and pituitary glands, viral diseases such as pneumonia and mononucleosis, cancer, and chronic cardiac conditions.

The second well-known dualistic concept of depression is *unipolar versus bipolar*. A diagnosis of unipolar depression is used when there is one or more episodes of depression alone. Bipolar depression (or manic-depressive illness) is diagnosed when there are episodes of both mania and depression. Bipolar depression is the type of disorder studied in the Amish community in Lancaster, Pennsylvania, where it was found to have a specific genetic link.

Currently, the most popular classification systems of depression are the *pluralistic systems,* which assume that there are many types of depressive disorders. The

American Psychiatric Association's *Diagnostic and Statistical Manual* (DSM-III), a diagnostic guide used by most mental health professionals, lists more than a dozen different types that vary in severity.

Finally, let's look at one model of diagnosis that combines many of the best aspects of these classification systems. Dr. George Winokur proposed a diagnostic procedure that follows a particular sequence. First, a clinician determines whether a depression is primary or secondary. Within primary depression, the depression is then separated into bipolar depression or unipolar depression. Within unipolar depression, there are three different kinds of depression:

1. Familial pure depressive disorder—depression in a person with a first-degree relative who also has depression.
2. Sporadic depression disease—depression in an individual with no first-degree relative who has a psychiatric disorder.
3. Depression spectrum disorder—depression in a person who has a first-degree relative who suffers from alcoholism or sociopathic problems (when a person does things that benefit himself or herself but hurt others, and that person does not care).

Winokur's sequence is summed up in the figure on page 104.

Winokur's classification system is of particular interest because of its focus on the familial prevalence of depression as one of the main criteria for diagnosis. With such information, it is easier for us to trace our family and genetic susceptibility to depression. Let's look at Susan's example again to see what her diagnosis

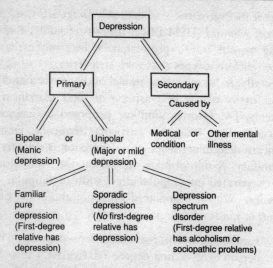

Figure 2. Winokur's Classification System.

would be in the Winokur classification system. We will also look at the DSM-III, by far the most widely used diagnostic system in the world.

As you recall, Susan was suffering from symptoms of depression, including insomnia, inability to concentrate, loss of appetite, and feelings of despair. As far as she knows, she does not have any other mental or physical illnesses, so her depression is a *primary* one. Within the category of primary depression, Susan's disorder can be considered *unipolar* because she has no symptoms of mania and only depression is present. Finally, since her mother apparently also suffered from depression, Susan's depression can be diagnosed as *familial pure depressive disorder* (depression in an individual with a first-degree relative who also has depression).

At this point, you may be thinking, "What difference does it make what the details of Susan's or anyone else's diagnosis are? Isn't it enough to know that she is depressed?" But it is important that you find out what the diagnosis is because that will determine the kind of treatment that you or your relative will receive. You know best what your symptoms of depression are, and how they have been affecting you. Having an understanding of the nature of your illness will help you to go to the right kinds of professionals so that you receive the correct treatment for the kind of depression that you have. In chapter 6, which explores treatment, these issues will be covered in more depth.

Diagnosis of Depression: How Does It Happen?

Depression is one of the most underdiagnosed disorders, primarily because it is frequently masked by other symptoms, including drug abuse and alcoholism. In addition, many of the symptoms of depression cannot be observed or assessed directly by medical professionals. Instead, the diagnosis of depression in made primarily on the basis of self-report. Since many physicians do not ask directly about symptoms of depression, unless the patient willingly offers that he or she has been suffering particular symptoms, depression frequently goes undiagnosed or misdiagnosed.

In response to the problem of "not asking the right questions," and in order to more accurately pinpoint the kind of depression an individual is experiencing, self-report symptom scales that define and clarify specific behaviors, feelings, and thoughts related to depressive episodes have been developed. Some of the inventories commonly used to measure depression are:

1. The Beck Depression Inventory—twenty-one groups of statements from which you are asked to select the one statement in each group that best describes the way you felt the preceding week.

2. The Minnesota Multiphasic Personality Inventory (MMPI) Depression Scale (D Scale)—several dozen true–false items such as, "Sometimes I feel I will never amount to anything."

3. The Lewinsohn Pleasant Events Schedule—a list of forty-nine activities. You are asked to indicate how often you engaged in each activity during the preceding thirty days, and to state how enjoyable each activity was on a 1- to 3-point scale.

The purpose of these inventories is to identify symptoms of depression when they might be hidden by other physical or mental illness diagnoses, and to determine the kind and the severity of symptoms. Again, these diagnoses are made through self-report, so the individual who denies that he or she is depressed is sometimes able to fool the professionals.

There is still no valid biological test for depression. Many people, instead of talking about feelings of hopelessness and loss of self-esteem, prefer to tell their doctors that they suffer from headaches, low energy, backaches, cramps, etc. One family doctor reported,

When I began asking all of my patients routinely if they had any symptoms of depression—and I had a list of the usual symptoms on a chart on the wall—I was astonished at the large number of people who reported that they had at least some of the symptoms of depression. And almost none of these people were in for a visit because of depression but rather for some physical ailment such as headaches, gastrointestinal problems, flu, or feeling tired. Their depression, which might have been the primary cause of their physical ailments, was ignored until I posted the chart of symptoms. I wonder just how many cases of depression go undiagnosed and untreated because we physicians are so busy treating the physical symptoms and missing the primary cause—depression?

Until 1980, when the *Diagnostic and Statistical Manual* (DSM-III) was published, doctors relied on their hunches or general impressions of depression to give a diagnosis. The DSM-III lists specific criteria that help doctors and other mental health professionals to identify depression in a systematic, uniform manner. The three criteria for identifying a major depressive episode are:

1. A relatively persistent "dysphoric" mood, characterized by anxiety, depression and restlessness, or loss of interest in pleasurable activities.
2. At least four of the following eight symptoms are present nearly every day for at least *two* weeks:

   • poor appetite or weight loss
   • insomnia or increased sleep
   • psychomotor agitation or retardation
   • loss of interest in usual activities

- fatigue or loss of energy
- feelings of worthlessness
- diminished concentration
- thoughts of death and suicide.

3. No evidence of mania, psychosis (impaired intellectual and social functioning with partial or complete
   loss of touch with reality), organic mental disorder,
   such as brain damage or tumor that resulted from a
   physical cause, or normal bereavement.

Everyone has some of these symptoms on occasion—
sleeping problems, feeling disheartened and disoriented,
being unable to feel pleasure, feeling self-pity. But the
difference between having these symptoms, even very
strong ones, now and then, and having these symptoms
persist for more than two weeks, is a big one. This difference is what separates run-of-the-mill depression that we
all occasionally experience from a serious depression.
When depression lasts longer than two weeks and the
symptoms are severe, then you need to be concerned that
you are suffering from serious clinical depression. And if
these symptoms do not go away, then you need to look
for help.

When Should You
(or Someone You Know)
Get Professional Help?

There are three situations that indicate the need for immediate evaluation and possible treatment by a mental
health professional.

Suicidal Feelings. The first situation occurs when you are feeling suicidal. When individuals feel suicidal, they are usually feeling very hopeless and in a great deal of anguish and pain. The pain may become so intense that the thought of ending it all by suicide seems to be a reasonable way of relieving the pain. It isn't. What has happened is that you (or the person with these feelings) have become seriously, dangerously depressed. When you are in this acutely painful, distorted state of mind, you cannot think rationally or reasonably. The risk of harming yourself is great when you are convinced that things are hopeless and there is nothing that can help you to alleviate the misery. Danny, a twenty-four-year-old student, described his feelings of depression and thoughts of suicide in this manner:

> No one could understand the great pain that I was feeling. I tried to tell my best friend, my parents, even my doctor, but no one could help me. It was as if I was on fire and no one could understand that they needed to help me douse the flames. And for some reason, I didn't know how to tell them. I suffered silently as the days went on. The fires continued to burn within me and I began to lose hope of ever feeling good again. I started to think about how good it would feel to end my life. It scared me at first but then it began to seem like a way out. Once I decided that I could kill myself anytime I wanted to, I felt almost jubilant. I felt like I had found the solution.

The young man who described his feelings did receive professional help in time to save himself from suicide, but many others are not so fortunate. It is estimated that about 15 percent of all depressed individuals commit suicide. Depression can be a serious, life-threatening illness.

If you have thoughts of killing yourself, you need professional help right away. Whenever you are convinced that your situation is hopeless, it's time to seek treatment, not suicide. If you are concerned that someone close to you is becoming depressed to the point of considering suicide, or showing signs of extreme withdrawal, persistent feelings of distress and misery, and problems communicating, try to talk to the person. You won't be able to cure the depression, but you can urge that person to seek professional help and possibly alleviate some of the terrifying feelings of isolation that sufferers of depression experience. In acute cases, sufferers are monitored 24 hours a day and sometimes put on antidepressant medication. They may receive intensive individual and group psychotherapy treatment, which acknowledges their pain, but also offers hope and support.

Serious Mental Disturbance (Delusional Thinking). The second situation in which an individual needs to seek immediate professional mental health treatment occurs when he or she has symptoms of a serious mental disturbance, such as delusional thinking. These people might believe that the world is plotting against them, or that bizarre, unknown forces are controlling their minds or bodies, or that voices inside their head are talking to them. Generally, they are losing touch with reality.

When this happens, an individual is usually said to be experiencing a psychotic episode, indicative not merely of depression, but of schizophrenia or another serious mental disorder. In most situations, individuals who have such symptoms are convinced that they are the only ones who are rational and that nothing is wrong with them. In fact, if you tell them that they need help, they will likely believe that you are part of the conspiracy to harm them. Most individuals who have these delusions refuse to seek professional help. In these situations you may have to take strong measures to insure that a psychotic person receives help by bringing him or her to a secure hospital or clinical setting where he or she can be evaluated by competent mental health and medical professionals.

Patsy, twenty-seven, is an example of a young woman who was in the throes of a psychotic episode. She stopped going to her secretarial job because she was convinced that the dictation headphones she listened through contained voices that were giving her secret messages. The voices wanted to control her, telling her when and what to eat, and that she shouldn't sleep because she would be in danger if she slept. Patsy became a wreck from the lack of sleep. She also had symptoms of depression, crying, feeling sad, and losing interest in most activities. When her sister Maureen went to her apartment to find out why she hadn't been going to work, she found Patsy disoriented and very defensive. Maureen realized that Patsy needed help, even though Patsy angrily told her to mind her own business. Luckily for Patsy, her sister was firm and insisted on bringing her to a clinic for observation. During the evaluation, it became clear that Patsy was suffering from a major mental disorder. After a three-month treatment program, including antipsychotic medication and residential treatment, Patsy no longer suffered from her psychotic delusions. She was able to resume her life and her employment.

A note of caution here: Sometimes individuals fear that they are going insane. They have panic attacks in which their heart pounds quickly, and they feel like they are crawling out of their skin. If you feel that you are on the verge of insanity, you are probably not. It is more likely that these are symptoms of an anxiety disorder. While an acute anxiety disorder may be serious, usually ordinary anxiety is not serious, and is easily treated. It is the delusions of psychotic episodes, when an individual is convinced that the delusions are real, that are serious.

Symptoms of Mania. The third situation when you should receive immediate professional help is when you have symptoms of mania. When an individual feels manic, he or she is filled with great energy, self-confidence, and enthusiasm. The creative juices are flowing during this stage, and many successful writers and artists report increased productivity. It is almost as if the ideas just keep bubbling and flowing, and people feel intensely alive. Speech patterns of individuals in a manic phase are characterized by rapid speech, clinically termed "pressured speech." It is as if the person cannot stop talking, even if he or she tried. But manics have difficulty keeping their thoughts on one topic. They jump from association to association so quickly that listeners cannot keep up with them, and manic persons may become annoyed that those around them cannot understand what they are trying to convey. In addition to speech, physical activity frequently increases. A manic person is usually very animated and is unable to keep still. Manics pace around, sleeping very little, and seem to have great amounts of energy to do many, many things. The experience of being manic is as if everything is intensified many times over. Manic persons describe the manic phase as euphoric, intoxicating, and ecstatic, and are so pleased with this feeling that it is hard to convince them that they need help.

To make matters even more difficult, individuals have very poor judgment during the manic phase. They behave in impulsive, often reckless ways, without any thought or care as to the consequences of their actions. An example of this type of behavior includes a woman who put $12,000, her entire savings, on one hand of blackjack at the casino because she was convinced that she would never lose. Or a man who impulsively left his home and marriage to spend a week with a woman he just met on an airplane trip, spending $10,000 to rent a villa in Spain for their fling.

The high energy and excitement cannot be maintained for very long. The euphoric state may turn into uncontrollable delirium, which in its most extreme cases may require hospitalization; or it turns into the opposite of mania—depression. The type of depression that usually follows a manic state can be immobilizing. Where the manic person was once full of energy, he or she is now unable to function normally, completely drained and apathetic.

The good news about manic-depressive illness is that it can be treated very successfully with the drug lithium. Lithium has proven to be effective in controlling and preventing mood swings in those who have chronic manic-depressive illness. While it is not a cure, it can control the chronic pattern of highs and lows. Since there is a strong genetic component in manic-depressive illness, sometimes physicians will even prescribe lithium as a preventive measure for those with a strong family history of manic-depression.

What about Other Types of Depression: How Will I Know if I Should Get Help?

Aside from the major depressive episodes and manic-depressive illness, many people suffer mild to moderate depression. Mild to moderate refers primarily to the type of depression, most specifically, the *nature* and *duration* of the symptoms, and not necessarily to the intensity of the symptoms themselves.

Jane, twenty-eight, is an example of a person who suffers from mild depression. Most of the time she is active and efficient, gets going quickly and gets things done. Once or twice a year, she has what she terms "the blues," times when she feels lousy. Usually her "blues" coincide with September, around the time when she separated from her husband four years ago. She feels tired, is unable to get out of bed in the morning, and is weepy. These symptoms last about a week, after which time, Jane gradually begins to feel better, returning to work and to her normal active self. After the fourth episode, Jane had resigned herself to being depressed for one to two weeks a year. "Other people have a much harder time with depression," she rationalizes. "At least I feel relatively good the other fifty weeks a year."

Since Jane's depressive symptoms last less than two weeks and occur only once or twice a year, she is considered to be suffering from mild, not major or clinical depression. Her symptoms, while strong, are relatively short in duration. She feels miserable, but is not suicidal. She does not have the debilitating difficulties (such as acute insomnia, appetite depression, lethargy, extreme difficulties in concentration) that are found in clinically depressed individuals.

Yet Jane has received no professional help and has not yet been diagnosed by a physician or psychologist. Although Jane doesn't appear to be suffering from any other physical illness, it is still not known if her depression is of a primary or secondary nature. Her depression seems to be both cyclical and chronic. For individuals like Jane who have experienced more than one depressive episode, it is important to have a medical workup as well as a psychological evaluation.

There are a large variety of medical conditions that have many of the same symptoms of secondary depression during any given stage of the illness. Some of these medical conditions include (but are not limited to):

Diseases of the immune system:
  AIDS (acquired immune deficiency syndrome)
  Lupus erythematosus

Infectious diseases:
  Hepatitis
  Mononucleosis
  Epstein-Barr virus (EBV) infection
  Pneumonia

Neurological disorders:
  Alzheimer's disease
  Multiple sclerosis
  Parkinson's disease
  Epilepsy

Other disorders:
  Some cancers
  Graves' disease (hyperthyroidism)
  Hypothyroidism
  Syphilis
  Brain tumors
  Anorexia
  Bulimia

As you can see, this partial list of medical conditions that may result in some of the symptoms of depression is quite long. Fortunately, a complete physical examination, along with laboratory test results, will customarily reveal any of these medical conditions. For example, in Jane's situation, it is not until she has completed a physical examination and routine laboratory tests that prove to be unremarkable in their findings that she can be diagnosed as having a primary depressive episode.

Let's look at another example. Maria is a person who exhibited symptoms of depression along with a medical condition. At thirty-three, she was a healthy, vibrant actress who worked hard waiting for her "big break" in show business. Just when she had begun to achieve some small success in winning larger parts in productions, Maria found herself feeling very run-down. Once a positive, upbeat person, Maria starting feeling pessimistic. She found she lacked the energy to have dinner with friends or to go on long walks. At night, her body ached, and she experienced painful feelings of loneliness. When it was time for Maria to go to rehearsal, she could barely drag herself out of bed. She was bewildered; she just didn't understand why she was feeling so badly when she was finally achieving all that she had hoped for. Maria even began to wonder if there wasn't something to the "fear of success" theory. Maybe she was afraid to be successful. Finally, confused and scared, she heeded the advice of a friend to consult a physician. Routine blood tests indicated that Maria was suffering from mononucleosis, an infectious disease that was causing her to feel very tired. Mononucleosis not only causes people to feel run-down; in some individuals, it can also cause feelings of depression. Once Maria rested and began to recover from the mononucleosis, her depression lifted. Relieved to be her vibrant, active self again, Maria went on to successfully star in several plays.

Diagnostic Difficulties:
Masking Symptoms of Depression

Not only are symptoms of depression frequently misdiagnosed, masking medical conditions, but the opposite occurs even more frequently: depression itself is masked by other conditions. It is so common that many experts believe that masked depression is seen much more frequently by nonpsychiatric physicians than is actual clinical depression or manic-depression.

At this point you may think, "But the symptoms of depression seem so obvious. How often is the diagnosis of depression actually missed by a doctor?" Undiagnosed depression is very common; estimates indicate that one third of all depression is either misdiagnosed or undiagnosed. The medical profession, in fact, considers patients with undiagnosed depression among the most frequent users of medical treatment. Since patients rarely report depression as their chief complaint in primary care offices (they usually report a variety of physical problems, including pain or fatigue), it can easily be undiagnosed and thus untreated.

However, physicians do try to treat the reported symptoms, usually to no avail. As a result, both the doctors and the patients are frustrated at being unable to find a physical reason for the somatic symptoms. Try as they might, they are frequently unable to relieve the pain of a patient whose underlying problem is depression.

So it is important for you to be able to recognize the many guises that depression can take, and to be familiar with "masked depression," depression that is hidden under a completely different face. Adult depression is usually disguised by psychosomatic disorders such as headaches, chronic pain, ulcers, and digestive problems, among others. It is only upon further questioning by an astute physician that the patient reveals that not only has he been suffering from back pain, but he has also been feeling quite despondent. Once again, if the physician does not ask about the depressive symptoms, the masked depression may not be revealed.

Another problem with treating the psychosomatic disorder without focusing on the underlying depression is that it may result in a phenomenon known as "symptom substitution," which occurs when the reported disorder (such as severe headaches) is treated successfully but the underlying problem of depression is not treated. What usually happens is that another psychosomatic symptom will take its place because the irritant, depression, is still there. Proper diagnosis, of course, would lead to treatment of the depression, and consequently, the end of the psychosomatic symptoms.

Even more common than masked depression in the medical setting is masked depression in the social setting, where it takes the form of substance abuse and of "acting out" behaviors.

Alcohol is the substance most frequently used by individuals who are depressed. When use (and subsequent abuse) of alcohol begins to be a problem of its own, the underlying cause, depression, is often forgotten. Since there usually is a constellation of symptoms and problems associated with alcoholism, it is important that treatment of depression be included in the treatment of alcoholism. Many alcoholics are depressed and despondent—it is easier in these cases to spot the depression, but other alcoholics are angry and hostile—it is less likely that the underlying depression will be picked up in these situations.

Socially, depression may be masked by abuse of other substances besides alcohol, including food (either overeating or eating disorders such as anorexia and bulimia), tobacco (persistent smoking or chewing of tobacco), and drugs such as marijuana, cocaine, crack, and heroin.

Anorexia nervosa is an eating disorder characterized by a distorted body image. The majority of anorexics are female. An anorexic is convinced that she is much fatter than she really is, and has an intense fear of becoming fat. In her striving for perfection, she loses up to one third of her weight, and is sometimes at risk medically because of such acute weight loss.

Bulimia is another eating disorder, characterized by binging (eating huge amounts of food) followed by purging, usually by vomiting and/or abuse of laxatives.

Research studies on the relationship between anorexia, bulimia, and depression have consistently found that a large number of individuals diagnosed as anorexics and bulimics also exhibit many symptoms of depression, including low self-esteem, feelings of hopelessness, insomnia, and dissatisfaction with one's body image. The optimal treatment for someone who suffers from both an eating disorder and depression is to treat both aspects of the illness. Sometimes the underlying depression can be masked by the medical urgency of the eating disorder. Once an individual's medical condition is stabilized, it may be important to treat the emotional symptoms of depression along with the anorexia.

Glenda, fourteen, is an adolescent girl with anorexia. The youngest of four children, Glenda always considered herself the "baby" of the family. She was friendly and seemed happy until she turned thirteen. After her birthday, Glenda became very concerned with her weight. Although she had always been slim, Glenda began to go on one diet after another in her desire to lose more weight. It became an obsession with her to try to eat less and less. When her family suggested to her that she was overdoing the weight loss, Glenda became angry.

Glenda began to withdraw into her own world, refusing to interact with anyone other than her few closest friends, who, she said, "understood her need to be thin." After her parents found her riding an exercise bicycle in the middle of the night, they insisted that she go to a psychologist. Reluctantly, Glenda did see a therapist, but she was generally uncooperative in her sessions. She continued to eat very small amounts of food and became thinner and thinner. One day at school, Glenda fainted and was taken to the hospital, where she was admitted to the children's psychosomatic unit. There, a complete psychiatric and medical evaluation indicated that she was suffering from anorexia, had an extremely distorted image of her body (she described herself as being "chunky" when in fact she was very thin), and had several symptoms of depression. These symptoms included lack of self-confidence, loss of touch with reality, extreme sadness, and suicidal feelings. She had two wishes—to "remain a baby" and to be loved by her family.

Glenda's case is not an unusual one for adolescent girls who are diagnosed as anorexics. She was hospitalized for three months, during which time her entire family came weekly to the hospital for family therapy sessions. Glenda also received intensive individual and group psychotherapy treatment, and was relieved to discover that she was not alone—that there were other girls her age who shared her fears about growing up, gaining weight, and who also felt very depressed. After her discharge from the hospital, Glenda and her family continued to attend family therapy sessions to help themselves establish new, positive ways of interacting and showing affection. The road to recovery was slow for Glenda and her family, but as her sense of self-esteem improved, so did her outlook on life. It has been one year since her fainting spell, and although Glenda still has days when she feels hopeless, those days are becoming fewer and fewer. Her prognosis is good for a complete recovery.

Females tend to mask their depression through eating disorders and psychosomatic illnesses, but there appear to be differences in the ways that males mask their depression. Males are more likely to display acting out behaviors, including violent outbursts, gambling, sexual acting out behavior (including promiscuity), and obsessively exercising or working.

As you can see, the way males mask their depression tends to be through action or activity. One psychological theory suggests that boys and men in our society are far more comfortable with being active, even when depressed, than being passive. Girls and women, on the other hand, have been socialized into being more passive and tend to turn their depression inward toward themselves, focusing on their own perceived inadequacies (such as their weight or being ill).

A psychiatrist who works with first-time criminal offenders remarked that the overwhelming majority of his caseload is made up of men, both young and old, whom he would diagnose as being depressed. In his experience, males who are depressed often commit crimes for the first time because they are feeling desperate and helpless. For some, committing a crime may seem like a way to fight depression because risk taking can be exciting; for others, participating in a crime may reflect the despair and hopelessness they feel. Or the act of committing a crime may be a cry for help.

Most remarkable is that most of these men usually deny being depressed when they are initially asked about their emotional well-being. It is only after they are required to describe their feelings in depth, and usually with the help of a self-report inventory or self-test, that they begin to admit to others and to themselves that they are experiencing feelings of depression.

Charles, forty-one, is an example of a man who became increasingly desperate and despondent after he lost his job. A master carpenter, he had been very proud of his work and his ability to support his family. Several months ago, Charles developed a serious ear infection that resulted in his losing his balance. He was unable to work at his job for weeks, and doctors did not know when he would be able to regain his balance again, if ever. If Charles was depressed about this setback, no one was able to tell by his behavior. He seemed to remain cheerful and kept busy by watching sports on TV, playing with his children, and hanging out with his buddies in the evenings. Two months after he became unable to work, everyone, including his family, was shocked when he was arrested for the armed robbery of a gas station. On a hunch, Charles's attorney asked him to undergo a full psychiatric evaluation. Both the psychiatrist and the psychological test data reported a diagnosis of a major depressive episode. In the interview, Charles remarked that he had been trying hard to pretend that he wasn't depressed or upset, to the point where he even felt he had fooled himself. Yet in a moment of despair he decided to take action and held up the gas station. It was an action he knew he would later regret. Ironically, though, it did ultimately result in his receiving help for his depression.

Charles's story is a typical one for men like him who become depressed and then act "out of character." Other common types of acting out behaviors that mask depression include excessive alcohol and drug use, as well as excessive physical activity, such as working out with weights for several hours a day. Because men who have masked depressive symptoms tend to demonstrate just the opposite of the usual symptoms of depression, a correct diagnosis is sometimes missed.

Accurate diagnosis of depression and other psychiatric disorders, as you can see, is sometimes easier said than done. There are many ways in which an incorrect or a missed diagnosis can occur. Symptoms of depression and other disorders, as well as symptoms of physical illness, may overlap. You may be diagnosed as having primary depression when in fact, you are unknowingly suffering from a physical illness which in its early stages mimics the symptoms of depression (you are probably suffering from secondary depression). Unfortunately, there is no easy laboratory test that can provide conclusive evidence of depression. In addition, each individual's experience of depression is unique, so a number of symptoms must be considered when screening a person for depression.

In spite of the many difficulties in correctly diagnosing depression, and the seeming vagueness of some of the testing methods, I must stress the importance of an appropriate diagnosis, so that you are correctly treated for psychological as well as physical disorders.

To summarize, a physician, psychologist, or other mental health professional has the tools for diagnosis that you are now familiar with:

1. The individual's self-report of symptoms, sometimes in the form of a self-test or self-report inventory.
2. A comprehensive family background and history, perhaps using a genogram to detect any genetic predisposition to depression.
3. Reported and observable behavior, with a special focus on lethargy, hyperactivity, and eating/sleeping problems.
4. An evaluation of the environmental stresses that the individual has been experiencing in the recent past.

With the information gathered in a thorough diagnostic evaluation, both you and the professionals have a good chance of making a proper diagnosis and increasing your chances of receiving the most effective treatment.

6

Treatment for Depression

When do you need treatment? The answer—when you or someone you know is too depressed to "just snap out of it," or you display only mild depressive symptoms, but you know that you have a family history of depression. If this is the case, you should seek preventive treatment even with mild-to-moderate symptoms *before* the depression becomes more severe. What kinds of treatment for depression are available? In the past two decades, a number of new and innovative methods have been developed for the treatment of depression, with some promising results. Treatments are now much more specialized and individually matched to the specific type of diagnosis, and with so many more resources and treatment techniques available, an estimated 80 to 90 percent of depressed people should benefit significantly. At the same time, however, it is estimated that fewer than 20 to 25 percent of the seriously depressed have been properly diagnosed and treated. Thus, it is important for individuals to take an active role in their own diagnosis and treatment, as well as in that of a friend or family member, beginning by acquiring a basic knowledge of the different kinds of treatment available.

In this chapter, you will find out about the types of treatments for depression, how each treatment is supposed to work, and the way it is usually determined which technique will be most effective for a particular type.

Here's a note of caution, though. This chapter is only an overview of information. If you are taking any of the medications or participating in a therapy treatment discussed in this chapter, this information should just serve as a starting point for you. You should get more detailed information about your specific type of treatment from your clinician. In particular, you need to familiarize yourself with the potential side effects of any medication you are taking.

Let's assume that you or someone you know is depressed enough so that it's impossible to "just snap out of it." How do you get professional help? There seem to be so many different mental health professionals, ranging from psychiatrists and psychologists to clinical nurses and social workers. Which should you choose? Or should you just go to your family physician?

The first and most important consideration in finding professional help is to get a proper diagnosis. It is usually necessary to undergo a complete set of laboratory tests and to have a full medical examination to rule out the possibility of a medical condition that might mimic the symptoms of depression. Initially, then, you should go to a medical doctor who can perform these tests.

After you have eliminated the possibility that you have a medical condition and you determine that your diagnosis is, indeed, depression, there are several options available.

The first may be to continue to be treated by your family practitioner. Many people are reluctant to see a psychiatrist or other mental health professional because of embarrassment and fear of being stigmatized. In addition, insurance plans generally have better coverage for medical conditions than for psychiatric conditions. While this may seem the easiest and most convenient option, it is not recommended that you receive treatment for depression from a general practitioner; you need specialized treatment from mental health professionals who are experienced with the nature of affective (emotional) disorders such as depression, know how to make a useful and specific diagnosis, and are familiar with the types of medications that are effective in the treatment of your particular kind of depression. These mental health professionals (sometimes also called psychotherapists) are:

1. Psychiatrists, or physicians with medical degrees (M.D.'s) whose specialty is in psychiatry (the medical study, diagnosis, treatment, and prevention of mental illness). Psychiatrists are the only professionals who can prescribe medications, and are generally also the only clinicians who can admit patients to an inpatient hospital for treatment.

2. Clinical psychologists with Ph.D. degrees, who are trained in the evaluation and treatment of mental illness. Psychologists are the only professionals who per-

form psychological and personality testing used in diagnosis and treatment.

3. Clinical social workers, with M.S.W. degrees (Master of Social Work), who are also trained in the evaluation and treatment of mental illness. Social workers frequently specialize in working with families, groups, or individuals in treatment.

4. Clinical nurses with nursing degrees (R.N.'s) who receive training on psychiatric units in clinics and hospitals to work with psychiatric patients. Nurses frequently administer and monitor medications, although they do not prescribe medications.

Each of these mental health practitioners has his or her own special function, but there is one shared responsibility—each can provide psychotherapy treatment. Therefore, when you hear the term psychotherapist, it can apply to any of these clinicians. The type of psychotherapy that each provides varies according to the particular discipline and the theoretical approach. Theoretical approaches differ according to the following behavioral influences: unconscious wishes and motivations (psychoanalytic approach), mind set and thinking (cognitive approach), learning theory (behavior approach), biochemical and neurological aspects of mental illness (medical approaches).

So there are different options in both personnel and approach, but many professionals work together in clinics and hospitals in a team approach in which each specialist may help to provide a different aspect of your care. Even private practitioners who work independently usually have a referral network of colleagues in other disciplines and specialities with whom they can collaborate on a particular person's treatment.

As noted earlier, if your medical doctor examines you and thinks it is necessary, he or she will refer you to a mental health professional. If you are severely depressed or actively suicidal, to the point where the physician thinks that you might need hospitalization, then you will most likely be referred to a psychiatrist. If you have clear symptoms of manic-depressive illness, you may also be referred to a psychiatrist for lithium treatment.

If you are treated by a psychiatrist, he or she can prescribe and monitor medication during the course of your visits. Or, if your symptoms of depression are less severe, you may see a psychologist, social worker, or clinical nurse for psychotherapy treatment alone. In a third and increasingly popular alternative, you may see a psychiatrist for medical treatment in conjunction with individual therapy from a psychologist or social worker, who might also work with your family as a unit.

Doesn't it make more sense to receive all your care from one person? Not necessarily. First, while some psychiatrists provide psychotherapy treatment, others may focus primarily on medication consultations and emergency situations, or work primarily in hospital settings.

In addition, there may be financial considerations. The hourly charge for a private psychiatrist's consultation or treatment averages $80 to $125; clinical psychologists charge $60 to $100; and social workers charge $40 to $80. Don't be alarmed by these seemingly high figures for private professional fees, however. If you have a comprehensive health insurance policy, it will usually cover part of your psychiatric costs, but it all depends on your particular plan. Many people are surprised to find that while virtually all costs of medical visits are covered by insurance (usually between 80 and 100 percent of the cost of a visit), the coverage for mental health care may be more limited. In a few states, insurance plans may not provide coverage for mental health services at all, or there may be a ceiling, or limit ($500 to $1,000 in most states) on the amount of outpatient therapy covered by most health insurance plans, including HMOs (health maintenance organizations).

Ironically, the most expensive mental health cost, hospitalization, is covered by insurance plans most thoroughly, while outpatient psychotherapy services for the less-debilitating forms of mental disorders are covered the least. Unless your insurance policy is very comprehensive, private clinicians' fees can amount to a large sum of money quickly.

What are other alternatives? Medicare, the program run by the Social Security Administration for people over sixty-five and for disabled people, and Medicaid, federal- and state-funded public assistance for low income persons who have no health insurance, offer minimal mental health benefits. Medicare usually pays for only 80 percent of the amount they allow for office visits and has limits on outpatient benefits. Medicaid will pay for 100 percent of mental health treatment, but the reimbursement given to clinicians and hospitals is very low, usually well below customary fees. As a result, it is sometimes very difficult to find a physician or hospital who will accept a Medicaid patient.

Many mental health clinicians do have sliding fee

scales that allow patients to pay according to their income. Clinics (both public and private) may provide comprehensive services, including medical consultations, prescription drugs, psychotherapy, and group support based upon ability to pay.

In addition, publicly funded community mental health clinics are found in most areas of the nation and serve people who live within a particular catchment area. The quality of service at these clinics varies, much as the quality of care you receive at any private practioner's office might vary. It is up to you to assess the quality of care based on referrals from others and from your own experience of the kind of care you receive.

Some medical schools or universities have clinics that are specifically focused on the study of depression. Sometimes they conduct research studies that examine the effectiveness of different kinds of treatment for depression. It may be possible to receive treatment at these depression clinics at little or no cost if you meet the qualifications (usually depending on your diagnosis, and sometimes demographic factors such as age and gender) of the subject population that the researchers are looking for.

At teaching institutions such as medical schools and university hospitals, you might be treated by an intern or trainee who has limited experience but who is supervised by experienced teachers. The cost for these types of services is low, but again, the quality can vary. Usually they are worth looking into if they can be found in the area where you live.

What should you look for when you consult with any mental health professional? First, you should try to find someone who is experienced in the treatment of depression and other affective (mood) disorders. You can start by asking your family physician for a referral. You can also contact your state psychiatric or psychological association and ask them for names of clinicians who specialize in the treatment of depression. Try to get two or three suggestions because it can be helpful to interview more than one person.

Let's assume that you are given two referrals. Now what should you say when you call? First, you should introduce yourself and say that you are seeking a mental health professional for an initial screening and treatment of depression. If you were referred by someone, you should say who referred you. The call to set up the interview is very brief; you do not go into details about your symptoms now but wait until the initial interview.

The Initial Interview

The initial interview is usually a conversation in which you and the clinician gather information about each other. He or she might ask you a number of descriptive questions about your symptoms, such as how long you've experienced them and how they have affected your normal functioning, about any personal or family background of depression or mental illness, and about your personal medical history and whether you have been taking any drugs (including medication of any kind). In addition, he or she may ask you to describe what has been going on in your life recently, such as any stresses, changes, losses, or other possibly upsetting events that might have triggered the depressive episode. Other topics that are commonly discussed are the nature and quality of your relationships with other people; what kinds of support you have; and what role family or friends might play in your treatment.

In the beginning, you might feel uncomfortable disclosing such sensitive and personal information to a stranger. Mental health professionals are accustomed to an initial hesitancy and will be sensitive to this, helping you to feel more comfortable as the session progresses.

You will also have an opportunity to ask the mental health professional about his or her training and experience working with people who are depressed, fees, and any other points that might relate to your own case, such as the possibility of family treatment and knowledge of antidepressant medication.

You will also have the opportunity to ask the clinician questions about his or her theoretical approach to treatment. Whether you are interviewing the therapist for yourself or for someone close to you, find out:

- How does the therapist go about understanding the causes of the depression, and what kinds of techniques will be used to treat depression?
- Does the therapist specialize in long or short term treatment or in any particular method of treating depression?
- What is the therapist's view on involving family or friends in treatment?
- How many sessions does the therapist expect family members to participate in?

- Does the therapist prescribe antidepressant medication or work together with a psychiatrist who does?
- What role does the therapist take in treatment, and what is expected of the client and the client's family?

These are some of the questions that will help you determine whether you want to work with a particular therapist. You should feel comfortable with the professional you choose, and asking questions at the outset can help you make sure you understand the treatment process.

If at all possible, it is a good idea to interview two or three professionals to find the best person for you to work with. You should trust your own impressions; you should like, respect, and be reassured by your clinician, and yet he or she should be someone who will challenge you to do your part in improving the way you feel.

You've Picked Your Clinician: Now What?

The initial interview is just the beginning of what could be considered the diagnostic phase, during which a great deal of background information is gathered so that the clinician can make an accurate diagnosis. It can commonly take from one to five sessions to complete the diagnostic process. This doesn't mean, however, that you won't receive any help for your depression until after the diagnostic procedure is completed. Depending on your symptoms, a psychiatrist might consider prescribing an antidepressant medication right away, in the hope of alleviating your symptoms. Or a clinician might recommend that you receive psychotherapy ("talk" therapy) to help you to understand and work on your problems. This could be in conjunction with medication, or entirely on its own. The reverse, however, is rarely true. That is, a doctor will seldom embark on a program of drug therapy when it is not accompanied by psychotherapy. There is still much that is not known about the effects of antidepressants, and doctors usually insist on close monitoring of any patient taking such medication.

Depending on your particular situation, the theoretical orientation and focus of your therapist, and what you are capable of doing in your own treatment, your doctor might start you on a program of cognitive therapy, or behavioral modification, or even an exercise program in order to help you get moving and feel better. Sometimes families, friends, lovers, and spouses can be included in your treatment program; they usually prove to be very helpful to both therapists and patients.

The Role of Family and Friends in Treatment

The participation of family and close friends in the treatment program of a depressed individual is important because it serves three major functions: (1) to educate and inform the family of the diagnosis, treatment plan, and progress, (2) to allow the family to help the "client" get better, and perhaps most importantly, (3) to offer the family supportive help and acknowledgment as to how difficult it has been to have a depressed person in the family system.

By the time the depressed person and the family have consulted a therapist, many things may have already gone wrong. The interpersonal relationships within the family, usually characterized by hostility, criticism, and avoidance, are likely to be strained because of the client's illness. Therapists can be helpful in suggesting techniques that help to change the nature of the interactions to become more supportive and positive. Since this can be hard to do without outside intervention, family therapists often encourage the entire family to attend a number of sessions in order to help them achieve a better relationship.

In addition, therapists may focus more specifically on the "primary" relationship of the depressed individual (the marital relationship or an intimate relationship with a "significant other"), which can be much like the confidant relationship discussed in chapter 3. While this type of alliance can serve as a buffer against depression, once an individual is actually in the midst of a depressive episode, the relationship can suffer. When this occurs, the relationship may be lacking in support, comfort, and understanding. The goal of therapy that engages the couple in treatment is to assist in developing the intimacy again. It has been found that the ability to reestablish a positive intimate relationship is vital to treatment as well as to the prevention of future depressive episodes.

While all of these treatment goals sound reasonable and helpful, they do require a great deal of hard work. Frequently, the spouse and family of a depressed person are frustrated, angry, and feeling hurt themselves. In addition, they have been deprived of the depressed person's help and support, so they, too, may be feeling needy. Because of these factors, it can be even more essential to find a therapist who includes the family in treatment.

You might be thinking, "This sounds good, but how does treatment really work?" To answer that, let's look at Susan again.

As you might recall, during Susan's depression, she was still going to work, but was accomplishing nothing. She avoided talking to her husband, Tim, because she didn't think she had the energy to tell him what was happening to her. Even if she could gather enough energy to talk to him, she doubted that he would understand. Tim was always so sure of himself, so busy, and so happy, that Susan was afraid he would think less of her if she told him how awful she felt. These feelings are typical of relationships in which one partner in a couple is depressed. There is usually reduced contact and communication.

On Tim's part, he was certainly not unaware that something was wrong with Susan. She just didn't seem her usual self. When Tim tried to talk to her about it, she became defensive, so he decided to back off. Tim felt bad, though, and helpless about what to do to make things better. (In time, the feelings of helplessness can turn into anger. If the anger is expressed to the depressed partner, it can contribute to the loss of self-esteem and hopelessness that the depressed person already feels.)

Three weeks went by, and things only got worse. Susan couldn't bear to go to work and face colleagues with her failure to accomplish anything, so she called in sick. When Tim suggested that she see a doctor, Susan told him to leave her alone. Stung by her rejection of what he considered to be his way of being helpful, Tim exploded in an angry tirade, telling Susan how fed up he was with her selfish behavior. Susan was devastated by his anger. She had been so preoccupied with her own problems that she hadn't even noticed what Tim was feeling or doing. She realized that the situation was now quite desperate. The memories of her mother's depressive episodes haunted her, and the fear that the same thing could happen to her finally prompted her to get help.

Susan was scared and her voice was shaking as she called her personal physician to ask him for a referral for help with her depression. She described her symptoms and was relieved when her doctor gently reassured her that she was sure Susan would be able to get help. After Susan contacted the two names she was given and set up appointments for interviews, she felt drained but also relieved. Maybe she wasn't quite so hopeless after all.

Susan talked to two different clinicians over a week's time. Both of them seemed competent, but she felt more comfortable with the second psychologist. After two diagnostic interviews and a medical evaluation with her regular physician that showed no medical conditions that would account for her symptoms of depression, the psychologist sent her to a psychiatrist for a medication consultation. Since the referral included the psychologist's diagnosis and summary of Susan's case, Susan was relieved that she did not have to go through her entire story again. The psychiatrist asked her a number of questions about her reaction to medications she had previously taken, her personal and family medical history, and her symptoms of depression. He prescribed a medication, Nardil, which he told Susan might take up to several weeks to have any noticeable effect. He then described the goal of the medication and informed her of a number of possible side effects, warning her to contact him immediately if she experienced any of the more dangerous ones. She was scheduled to meet with him on a monthly basis to monitor her reaction to the medication, in addition to continuing her weekly psychotherapy sessions with her psychologist.

Susan's psychologist explained that the most effective treatment for her would be this combination of medication and psychotherapy. Given Susan's family history of depression and other related disorders, it was likely that she had inherited a predisposition to depression and that her illness had a biological basis that could be treated with medication. However, because medication only addresses part of the problems associated with depression, Susan was a good candidate for psychotherapy treatment that would focus on issues of self-esteem, her feelings of guilt, and her relationship with Tim, among other personal and interpersonal issues.

There are different treatment options that Susan could take advantage of. In this particular situation, her doctors felt that her type of depression would respond well to a combination of medication and psychotherapy. Other clinicians might focus more on the family system, involving Tim more in her treatment, or focus *only* on psychotherapy rather than medication. In the past, clinicians generally focused on one form of treatment, but now different types are often combined. This combination of medication and psychotherapy is becoming more and more common in the treatment of depression. There is a growing recognition in the mental health field that an integration of both approaches is probably the most effective. As one National Institute of Mental Health (NIMH) official put it, "If a month or two has gone by and talk therapy isn't helping your patient's depression, it may be time to try drugs; just as psychotherapy can often help people taking antidepressants recover even more quickly."

In addition to individual psychotherapy, short-term therapy groups and self-help "Depressives Anonymous" groups have often been effective in treating depression. Short-term therapy groups, led by experienced therapists, give individual members the opportunity to share their personal experiences in the context of situational risk factors. These risk factors might be related to interpersonal relationships, financial issues, social issues and demands, etc.

Through group discussions, patients come to realize that their experiences, emotions, and depressive feelings are not at all unique. By validating their experiences and their reactions, group members establish common ground with each other and in so doing, feel less isolated. Ultimately, the group process enables the members to work together to find ways in which they can change their behavior to overcome their depression. This process allows both the member whose problems the group focuses on at any given moment *and* the supporters (other members of the group) to learn and to heal by participating in their own treatment and recovery.

In this way, self-help and support groups are also very helpful in providing a sense of support and encouragement for people who are depressed. Support groups are springing up in almost every city and town, and almost every hospital with a department of psychiatry or psychology can refer you to one of these self-help groups organized and run by depressed persons in various stages of recovery. As one participant of a Depressives Anonymous group said,

> I was doing much better in my treatment, but it was so affirming to be around other people who had experienced the same despair that I had. They understood and accepted me in a way none of my friends or even family could. My attendance in this group has helped me to fight my tendency to become depressed. If I miss a meeting, someone always calls me to find out how I'm doing and convinces me to go to the next one. After a meeting, I always feel better than when I came. I'm determined to beat depression, and the group support really helps.

Families of depressed people also carry a large burden, and self-help groups have been enormously helpful to those who have experienced the depression of someone they love. One group in New York is called Families of Depressives, and meets biweekly. The group lends support to spouses, lovers, parents, siblings, and children of depressed people in dealing with their anger, feelings of loss and resentment, and their frustrations with the sometimes slow recovery process. One husband of a depressed wife remarked,

> I'm not the patient, but I need help too. The family support group is the only place where I can complain about my wife's depression and people there will still understand that I love her. They know because they feel the same way about their own loved ones. We often have to be the strong, supportive ones at home, but here we can cry, too, and give each other strength.

Help *is* available, and in many different forms. When you feel desperate, or even suicidal, try talking to someone, anyone. Suicide hot-line phone numbers appear in virtually every phone book in the country. Check listings under "Suicide" or "Crisis Hot Line." Generally there is a trained volunteer at the other end of the line, ready to listen to your problems and help you through the roughs spots. These hot lines are not intended to treat your depression but are there to tide you over until you can seek professional help. In the Northeast, one of the largest groups that coordinates hot lines is the Samaritans. There are also special hot lines for teenagers (Samariteens, for instance) with phone workers who specialize in adolescent concerns. There are similar organizations nationwide.

Three Major Treatment Approaches: A Comparison Study

A recent NIMH-supported study examined the effectiveness of the three major treatment approaches to depression:

1. *Cognitive behavior therapy,* originated by Dr. Aaron Beck, which teaches patients to identify and change unrealistic, negative views of the world and of themselves, which contribute to and help to perpetuate the depression.
2. *Interpersonal psychotherapy,* originated by Dr. Myrna Wasserman, which focuses on helping depressed persons to improve their interactions with others, enabling them to get their emotional needs met much more effectively.
3. *Standard drug therapy,* with the medication Tofranil.

In the study, depressed subjects were assigned randomly to one of the three treatment programs for a period of four months. At the end of that time period, they were evaluated for symptoms of depression. Results indicated that all three treatment approaches dramatically improved the mood of the depressed individuals within the relatively short four-month time period.

The startling effectiveness of the three treatment approaches underscores what professionals have suspected all along—that focused, rapidly effective forms of psychotherapy, along with new discoveries in drug treatment (with fewer side effects than in the past), offer depressed people many more options for effective treatment.

Antidepressant Medications

Lithium for Manic-Depressive Illness

What are antidepressant medications, anyway? Antidepressant medications are not a *cure* for depression, but they can be an effective tool in the control of symptoms of depression and manic-depression. Not unlike many other medications, the effectiveness of most antidepressants, including the drug lithium, was first discovered accidentally.

The discovery of lithium's ability to control manic behavior is attributed to an Australian psychiatrist, Dr. John Cade, who, when investigating the effects of uric acid in 1949, inadvertently discovered that lithium (which had been combined with the uric acid to make it more soluble) produced a calm state in guinea pigs. Later that year, Cade reported that lithium was, indeed, successfully used to control mania.

Despite this early reported success with lithium, its use was not accepted in the United States until 1974, when the U.S. Food and Drug Administration (FDA) put lithium on its list of substances that could be prescribed for the prevention and treatment of manic-depression. Since that year, lithium has become widely accepted as the drug of choice in the treatment of patients with manic-depression and in some cases of recurrent major depression as well. It has been shown to be effective in alleviating symptoms in over 90 percent of manic-depressive patients.

The only tricky part of prescribing lithium is maintaining the correct dosage and insuring that the patient does not have any contraindications for lithium (such as problems with kidney functioning, as lithium needs to be eliminated from the body by the kidneys). Thus, all prospective candidates for a lithium trial need to undergo a complete medical evaluation, including laboratory tests to measure kidney functioning and thyroid hormone level. After lithium is prescribed, these tests are conducted at regular intervals, usually every three months or so.

Maintaining the proper concentration of lithium in the blood is a bit like performing a balancing act: too little, and there is no therapeutic effect; too much, and the lithium can be toxic. To walk that narrow line and determine just the right amount requires that blood tests be conducted so that, in the beginning, the lithium concentration in the bloodstream can be measured accurately every few days. While the dosage as well as the time it takes for the lithium to be effective varies from individual to individual, most people experience some relief from manic symptoms within one to two weeks. Once the level of the lithium in the bloodstream is stabilized and the proper dosage for the individual determined, blood tests can be conducted at longer intervals, up to a month apart. It is not an addictive drug, so treatment can be discontinued at any time.

Are there any side effects of lithium use? Unfortunately, almost all of the drugs prescribed for the treatment of depression have some side effects associated with them. With lithium, the risk of the most dangerous side effect, toxicity, is substantially reduced with continual monitoring of the level of lithium in the blood. Some people do experience minor side effects such as weight gain, slight hand tremor, thirst, and gastrointestinal problems, similar to what one might experience with aspirin use.

But the beneficial aspects of lithium for a manic-depressive far outweigh the potential side effects. It's not only effective in alleviating symptoms of manic-depression, it is effective in the prevention of further episodes. Thus, many individuals who have had recurrent problems with manic-depression may need to take lithium for the rest of their lives. Long-term use of the drug has been shown to be relatively safe.

The accidental discovery over forty years ago of lithium's effectiveness in treating manic-depression has made a vast difference in the lives of many people who had previously endured wildly fluctuating mood swings. It has allowed countless numbers of sufferers to live calm and productive lives.

Medications for Mild to Major Depression

The medications known as antidepressants and prescribed for the treatment of mild to major depression can be divided into three major groups: the *tricyclics,* the *MAO* (monoamine oxidase) *inhibitors,* and *Prozac.*

These three classes of drugs appear to work by affecting the brain's neurotransmitters (the chemical messengers that carry information from neuron to neuron).

More specifically, the tricyclics work by helping to expand the activity of norepinephrine, a neurotransmitter secreted by the adrenal glands. The MAO inhibitors also seem to work by increasing the concentration of norepinephrine in the bloodstream. Prozac works the same way as the tricyclics but exclusively on serotonin, another neurotransmitter.

How does this increase of norepinephrine or serotonin help to decrease depression? Simply stated, many scientists believe that depression may be caused by a deficiency of norepinephrine, while manic episodes might be attributed to an excess of it. If this is so, then antidepressants work by increasing the amount of epinephrine and serotonin in depressed individuals.

The tricyclic antidepressants, named for their three-ring chemical structure, include the following drugs:

Generic Name	Trade Name
amitriptyline	Elavil, Endep
imipramine	Tofranil
doxepin	Sinequan
trimipramine	Surmontil

The tricyclics are commonly the first drugs tried by psychiatrists when prescribing medication for depression. They do have side effects, which affect some people more severely than others, including drowsiness, dry mouth, nausea and dizziness, and blurred vision. As with all medications, different people react in different ways to a particular drug. Usually, some trial and error experimentation is needed before the right dosage and sometimes even the right drug is prescribed.

The MAO inhibitors include the following drugs:

Generic Name	Trade Name
phenelzine sulfate	Nardil
tranylcypromine sulfate	Parnate
isocarboxazid	Marplan

The MAO inhibitors are usually prescribed when individuals do not respond to the tricyclics or if they have heart disease and cannot be given tricyclics. They also seem to work well with those depressed people who have atypical symptoms of depression, such as overeating, extreme anxiousness, or sleeping for long periods instead of suffering from insomnia. The drawbacks of using MAO inhibitors include possible side effects of seizures, rashes, insomnia, and high blood pressure, in addition to a number of strict dietary restrictions. Persons taking MAO inhibitors must avoid most preserved and fermented foods such as cheese, sausages, pickles, overripe bananas, avocados, certain kinds of wine, and smoked meats and fish, among others. If these foods are eaten in combination with MAO inhibitors, there is a risk of a dangerous rise in blood pressure. Because of these dietary restrictions, MAO inhibitors are prescribed less frequently than the tricyclics, but they are sometimes effective in alleviating symptoms of depression when nothing else seems to work.

A number of new, faster-acting antidepressants—including Prozac—have come along in the past decade. While tricyclics and MAO inhibitors generally require two to three weeks to produce noticeable antidepressant effects, with some of the following new drugs improvement is reported in as little as four to five days:

Generic Name	Trade Name
amoxapine	Asendin
trazodone	Desyrel
alprazolam	Xanax
fluoxetine	Prozac

Asendin has a mild sedative effect but works quickly. Desyrel has fewer side effects than other antidepressant drugs but may cause persistent erection or impotence. Xanax is an antianxiety medication much like Valium; its use may result in dependence.

Prozac has become the most widely prescribed antidepressant drug since it was first introduced in December 1987. The advantage of Prozac is that it is easier to tolerate and it produces fewer side effects than the tricyclics and MAO inhibitors. Furthermore, its effectiveness is comparable to the traditional antidepressants but it requires less trial and error in determining the right dosage for each individual. Instead, a standard dose seems to work effectively for most people. In addition, Prozac has a broader range of use and has been effective in treating related disorders such as obsessive-compulsive behavior, anxiety, and—as some preliminary studies suggest—even drug addiction.

On the other hand, it is important to note that while Prozac has been hailed as a wonder drug, much of its longer-term effects are still unknown. As time passes and more clinical trials are completed, we will learn more about Prozac. Until then, it does appear to be a promising antidepressant drug with good performance potential.

As noted, all of these drugs have some side effects, and further research is being conducted to develop new, more effective medications while reducing undesirable side effects.

Electroconvulsive Therapy (ECT)

Decades ago, in the 1930s and 1940s, electroconvulsive therapy (ECT) was the only known treatment for severe depression. Doctors did not know how it worked, but they knew that a controlled electric current administered to the head induces a type of seizure that somehow jolted people out of a severe depressed state. But not only were they jolted out of a depression, ECT patients suffered memory loss and disorientation. Because of the memory loss, as well as the unpleasant associations with electric shock, ECT fell out of favor in the 1960s and 1970s. More recently, the medical profession has acknowledged its effectiveness in treating *severe* cases of depression. It has been shown to be particularly effective in situations in which the individual is *acutely suicidal* and the three weeks that it might take an antidepressant to take effect could mean the difference between life and death. In fact, once a patient undergoes a course of ECT treatment, suicides are very rare. However, ECT treatment is used only in the *most severe* cases, after all other options have been tried and exhausted.

While the problem of short-term memory loss is still a major concern with the use of ECT, some advances have been made. "Brain mapping" computers now help to guide the shocks to only one side of the head to reduce memory loss, and the electric currents are now briefer. Studies indicate that those who receive shocks on only one side of the brain regain their memory functioning within one to two months. Again, use of ECT is limited to the most severe cases of depression that have been unresponsive to other treatment. In these cases, it has been shown to have positive and life-saving results.

Other Treatments: Resetting the Biological Clock

In addition to the recent advances in drug treatment, shorter psychotherapy approaches, and improvements in ECT, the use of light therapy to treat SAD (see chapter 3) has resulted in a renewed focus on the role of sleep in depression.

The body's daily rhythms seem to play an important role in depression. Most people who suffer from major depression are at their worst in the morning, while manic-depressives feel worse toward the afternoon and evening. Trying to make sense of this information, scientists looked at the sleep cycles of depressed people and found that most depressed people take longer to fall asleep than the general population. They often wake up in the middle of the night, and they tend to wake up much earlier than nondepressed people.

Even more significant is the pattern of REM activity (rapid eye movement—the phase of sleep during which people dream) in depressed people. While a normal REM pattern begins 90 minutes after a person falls asleep, in depressed individuals, it begins much earlier, at 20 to 30 minutes. In addition, the entire pattern of sleep is different for depressed people. A healthy subject population experienced most of their REM periods during the last third of the night, while depressed populations had most of their REM periods during the first third of the night. The sleep patterns are so strikingly different between depressed and nondepressed individuals that some sleep labs measure the sleep patterns of patients to decide if a person is actually suffering from major depression or from a medical condition such as Alzheimer's disease, which mimics many of the symptoms of depression. If lab tests show that REM periods occur early in the night, it is much more likely that the patient is suffering from depression as opposed to a medical condition.

Scientists also found another very interesting fact. Depressed people who were somehow deprived of a night of sleep seemed to feel better the next day. Further sleep lab studies showed that it was not the lack of sleep that caused the uplift in mood, but the lack of REM periods. Unfortunately, eliminating REM periods proved insufficient for treating depression, because after one or two days, the depression returned. However, scientists are intrigued by the effect of sleep and sleep deprivation on hormone levels. They hope for the development of a new kind of drug treatment that might change the hormone levels of the sleep cycle. If the hormone levels and, subsequently, the REM periods of depressed people could be adjusted, this could mark a new advance in the treatment of depression.

Scientists are also just beginning to make advances in understanding the complex relationships between depression and cognitive, interpersonal, and familial factors. Light therapy and exercise therapy have been discovered only in the last decade or so. And in the near future, we will undoubtedly learn much more and be able to develop more effective treatments to help specific kinds of depression.

7

Depression in Women, Children, and the Elderly

Depression in Women

Sherry, forty-one, called in sick this morning for the third day in a row because she couldn't get herself out of bed. "I deserve to stay home," she thought to herself. "My body aches, my head hurts, and I feel lousy." As the day went on, Sherry began to feel more lonely and sad. "This is miserable," Sherry told her mother. "I'm going to the doctor. I must have the flu or a virus."

At the doctor's office, Sherry's physician listened attentively as she described her symptoms: headaches, back and neck pains, insomnia. He did a thorough physical exam and ordered a batch of laboratory tests. The next day, all the lab tests came back with negative findings. Sherry's doctor called her with the news, "I can't find anything wrong. Maybe you just need a little rest. Have you been under much stress lately?"

Sherry didn't know what to say. "No more stress

than usual." When she hung up, she began to cry. "I'm hopeless," she thought. "Even the doctor can't find out what's wrong with me."

Sherry may not know it, but she has plenty of company. In 1986, a study lead by Dr. Kenneth B. Wells, a psychiatry professor at UCLA's Neuropsychiatric Institute, looked at 11,000 medical patients who went to their doctors during a nine-day period. Like Sherry, the great majority of this group thought they were suffering from something other than depression. Overall, the study found that one in every five persons (and none of these were psychiatric patients) had significant symptoms of psychological distress such as sadness, insomnia, loss of interest in sex, change in appetite, and just plain feeling lousy for a month or more. Twice as many women as men reported these symptoms of depression. In many of these cases, not only was the depression unknown to the patients, but it was also undiagnosed by their personal physicians.

This study's findings confirmed previous estimates that 20 percent of a general (nonpsychiatric) population had many symptoms of depression. In addition, the study reported some interesting results: The researchers found that depression can be as disabling as other illnesses, such as serious heart disease. In fact, being depressed seems to cause as much disruption in everyday life as other major chronic medical conditions including diabetes, kidney disease, and heart disease.

The study reported that people who are depressed have an equally difficult time performing daily routine activities such as getting dressed, walking, climbing stairs, working and socializing with friends, as do people who have more easily recognizable chronic medical conditions.

The 2 to 1 gender ratio of depressed women to depressed men is a consistent finding, based on several different studies, putting women at a higher risk for the disabling effects of depression. This ratio is found in other industrialized Western countries, as well as the United States. Moreover, this higher prevalence is reported in both patient and nonpatient populations randomly surveyed in communities in different regions of the United States. The only known exceptions were found in studies of populations in some developing (nonindustrialized) countries and studies relating to manic-depressive illness, in which the gender ratio is close to 1 to 1.

Why is the depression rate for women twice as high as for men? This question has intrigued many mental health professionals as well as researchers. Several theories have been suggested to explain the gender difference in depression rates, but because no definitive answer or theory has emerged, several theories will be discussed here.

First, it was necessary to determine if the higher rate of depression among women is indeed a true finding; it is necessary to rule out the possibility that more women might be diagnosed as depressed because they are more likely to report it, or because they seek help more often. Since men are more likely to express their depression in different ways, it was also necessary to make sure that depressed men were not being misdiagnosed and undercounted.

In considering whether women go to doctors more

often or are willing to report symptoms more readily than men, researchers focused on surveys of the general population. (Very few had ever received psychiatric treatment, nor did they go to the doctor more often than the average person). Since the 2 to 1 ratio of depressed women to depressed men was also found in the general population samples, it is unlikely that increased utilization of health care alone could explain the higher incidence of depression among women.

In examining other factors that might account for this ratio, studies have shown that women do report symptoms of depression more frequently than men do. The theories that women might feel that it is more permissible for them to report depression or that they experienced more stressful life events than men did were examined, but were not supported by any findings. The conclusion was that more women reported symptoms of depression because more women than men were actually depressed.

There are two other explanations of why the 2 to 1 ratio might not reflect a true higher incidence of depression. First, some men who could be diagnosed as depressed are found in the criminal justice system, with antisocial behavior masking the symptoms of depression. This percentage is considered to be small, and is difficult to verify. Some researchers don't acknowledge this factor.

Second, since many more men have alcohol abuse problems than women, some cases of depression in men might be masked by alcoholism, and might be included in the alcoholism rates instead of the depression rates.

However, recent studies of the patterns of heredity show that the transmission of alcoholism and depression are independent; that is, while both depression and alcoholism may occur within the same individual, their patterns of *family transmission* are distinct. While there certainly are some men who are depressed but are diagnosed as alcoholic, their numbers are relatively small; if they were added to the category of depressed men, the size of this group still would not approach that of depressed women.

As a result, most researchers believe that the fact that women are twice as likely to be depressed as men is a true finding and not due to misdiagnosis, difference in utilization rates, or willingness to report depressive symptoms. Given this, several theories have been suggested to explain the difference in depression rates between genders.

Biological Factors

Initially, people focused on biological factors, questioning whether depression is passed on from mother to daughter, or whether females are more likely than males to inherit the "depression gene" from either parent. While evidence indicates that the predisposition to depression is inherited, the data does not show that females in the same family are more susceptible than males to inherit depression. In fact, inheritability is equal between males and females. So, genetic factors cannot explain the higher rate of depression among females, but do seem to be important in the transmission of depression and manic-depression for *both* females and males.

Another biological factor to be considered is the effect of female hormones and the role, if any, they might play in depression. Women have frequently reported feeling moodier during the premenstrual phase of their cycles. In addition, it has been a persistent belief that women who are menopausal feel more depressed. Is there any scientific basis to these reports?

To date, there is no conclusive evidence that female hormones or the hormonal balance is correlated with depression. There is some evidence that suggests that premenstrual syndrome (PMS) and use of birth control pills (which contain hormones such as estrogen) may increase the rate of depression in women. Studies that have measured these increases have found only small effects, however, nothing that would explain why large numbers of women are depressed at all different phases of their menstrual cycles. There was also no evidence to support the idea that menopause in any way increased the incidence of depression.

There was some evidence that many women did report symptoms of depression during the postpartum period, right after giving birth. Postpartum depression can take many forms, from feeling weepy and sad for a few days after childbirth to severe, debilitating depression that might last for several months and require hospitalization.

How serious a problem is postpartum depression? It's estimated that 50 to 70 percent of postpartum women experience a brief period of depression, sometimes called maternity blues. Most women experience this three to four days after giving birth, at the same time when lactation (breast milk production) begins. The symptoms include weepiness, often unpredictably and seemingly without reason; irritability; fatigue; a loss of self-confidence; and insomnia. These symptoms usually go away by themselves within a week. Unlike other forms of depression, there is virtually no risk of a relapse or reoccurrence of this type of depression (until the birth of another child, that is. And the risk is no greater for subsequent births.)

A much smaller group, an estimated 10 to 20 percent of postpartum women, experience a moderate to moderately severe depression, lasting from several weeks to several months. Their symptoms are similar to those of major depressive episodes, with loss of self-esteem, loss of interest in previously enjoyable pursuits, physical complaints, feeling overwhelmed, and an inability to concentrate and function. What makes this type of depression unique and different from "regular" depressions is that the woman will feel extreme anxiety about the baby's well-being and have debilitating self-doubts about her capacity to be a "good, nurturing mother." These self-doubts can be so strong that a new mother may feel overwhelmed to the point of being unable to function. A vicious cycle is then created, as the woman feels incompetent, then is unable to function, then feels bad about herself because she is unable to function, and so on. Usually, a woman in this situation requires supportive individual and group counseling to help get her "unstuck" from this cycle and to view the situation more positively so she can help herself.

Hannah, a social worker who runs a supportive therapy group for new mothers, describes what happens in the groups that she leads:

> In the beginning, no one admits to negative feelings toward their babies. The mothers all rave about how cute they are and how much they love them. As the group continues and I ask about how the babies have changed their lives, they start to admit that yes, the baby is a burden, or yes, they wish they could have some time alone without a demanding child nearby. Eventually, one brave woman will say, "I don't think I'm a very good mother." And the entire group will nod and agree with her, relieved that they are not alone in feeling that way. I think if we could demystify motherhood and the illusion that "good" mothers never wish to get away from their children, new mothers would do much better because they wouldn't feel so alone and guilty. If you can get rid of the guilt, you'd go a long way toward treating the depression.

There is a very small percentage of postpartum women, one-hundredth of one percent, or 1 in 10,000 women, who experience a debilitating psychotic illness after giving birth. These are the rare cases that make headline news, when a new mother suffers extreme postpartum depression and becomes so overwhelmed that she abandons or otherwise harms her baby. These cases are very small in number. Women who are at the highest risk for psychotic postpartum depression are women who have a history of manic-depressive illness or previous psychosis.

Since a change in hormonal levels does seem to cause

postpartum depression or "the maternity blues," could this account for the greater numbers of women who are depressed? Probably not, since it is only in specific situations such as childbirth that hormonal levels change so dramatically. However, this is a new area of research and further studies of the hormonal levels of depressed women might give us more information for developing new treatments.

Environmental Factors: The Social Status Theory

Much attention has been focused on the environmental or social factors that might contribute to the high rate of depression among women. The social status theory suggests that long-standing social discrimination and the resulting low social status of women may help to explain why women are depressed. The theory assumes that women find their situation depressing because real social discrimination makes it more difficult for them to succeed. It focuses on several social factors:

First, the role of women in the United States, as well as in other industrialized countries, is still more restricted than men's roles. In spite of the many legal and social advances women have gained in the past century, opportunities for financial, social, and career fulfillment are still fewer than for men of equal education. Women in the labor market occupy jobs with lower salaries and lower status and have less authority than men. In addition, studies have shown that women have fewer opportunities for promotion and job advancement.

Second, these inequities in opportunity can cause women to feel helpless, particularly with regard to their financial situation and supporting a family, resulting in a dependency on others and a loss of self-esteem. Once an individual feels helpless and lacks self-confidence, depression may not be far behind.

While these social and environmental factors refer specifically to women's roles and discrimination, the same concepts can be applied to members of ethnic minority groups in this country, as many of the issues of discrimination and social status are the same. Like women, members of ethnic minority groups in this country, such as black Americans, Native Americans, Asian Americans, and Hispanic Americans, have higher rates of depression when compared to the white majority population. It is likely that people who have a "double" discrimination status, such as a Native American woman, may be at an even higher risk.

Environmental Factors:
The Learned Helplessness Theory

The learned helplessness theory suggests that men and women are socially conditioned to accept the stereotypical image of gender behavior in our society. The stereotypical role for a woman is one in which she is dependent and helpless, wants to be taken care of, and feels inadequate. These classic values of femininity are very similar to those of the learned helplessness theory, which proposes that individuals learn that whatever they do makes little difference—the outcome is not under their control—and have a resigned, helpless attitude. In other words, they give up. When applied to women, this theory suggests that women have learned not only to give up their independence and control, but to give up altogether, reflecting the social conditioning that takes place as girls develop into women, and helps to explain why women are twice as likely as men to be depressed.

How valid and useful are these theories when applied to real life situations? I interviewed a psychotherapist who leads several therapy groups for depressed women. She gave two examples of women whom she feels are depressed because they learned to be depressed through social conditioning:

> Charlene, forty-four, had just gotten a divorce when she joined my therapy group. She was a successful real estate agent with two daughters, both doing very well in college. Charlene, attractive and well-dressed, looked like the picture of success. Why would *she* be in a group for depressed women? In the beginning, it seemed as if she didn't know the answer either. All she knew was that she felt miserable. As other women shared their fears of being lonely, or being failures, Charlene nodded in understanding. She, too, was scared to death of living alone, without a husband and children, for the first time in over twenty years. Having played the role of the "super achiever" all her life, being the perfect mother, wife, and still running a successful business, Charlene now felt betrayed. She had given of herself to everyone else, even taking responsibility for her elderly mother, and had neglected to learn how to take care of herself. Charlene didn't have a clue as to who *she* really was, what she wanted, and how to please herself. She was empty, depressed, and needed to start all over again. The

therapy group helped her to understand this; in time, she became one of the leaders of the group, helping newcomers identify *their* issues.

Charlene is one of the many separated and divorced women who make up the largest category of depressed individuals. Studies have shown that women are much more likely to become depressed in a failed marriage or relationship. In fact, many women's depressions are precipitated by the specific events that are causing the problems in the relationships. When these women were compared with an otherwise similar group of divorced, nondepressed women, there were no demographic factors that differentiated them, which suggests that it is the events leading to divorce that resulted in depression in these women.

When researchers studied a group of depressed divorced men to see if it is also the events leading to divorce that result in depression for men, they found different answers than they did for women. Depressed divorced men, when compared with an otherwise similar group of nondepressed divorced men, did have demographic variables that differentiated them from the nondepressed group. The depressed divorced men had histories of interpersonal difficulties and a variety of problems with their sexuality, factors that were not present in the comparison group of nondepressed divorced men. This finding suggests that, among men, the symptoms of depression likely preceded the divorce and the depression may have been a factor in causing the divorce. On the other hand, for *women,* the depressive symptoms likely come *after* the divorce and the divorce may have been a factor in causing the depression.

These findings are consistent with the theory that social and interpersonal inadequacies are a major risk factor for depression for women. It has long been suspected that men and women become depressed for different reasons. A study of college students found that the main reason that female students become depressed was a breakup of an intimate relationship. For male college students, the main reason for depression was perceived personal failure, such as academic failure or failure in extracurricular activities, such as sports.

As a result, women are very dependent on other people, particularly on their partners in intimate relationships, for their emotional well-being. Women who do not have a supportive social network of friends and family or who are not involved in a meaningful intimate relationship are at higher risk for depression. The same is not true for men, who are far less dependent on either a supportive social network or an intimate relationship for their emotional well-being. The men who are at higher risk for depression than other men are those who judge their own personal achievements in their careers as being inadequate.

Other Risk Factors
Let's get back to our psychotherapist who is leading the therapy group for depressed women. She has another example to illustrate some other risk factors for depression in women.

Tina, thirty-two, is a single mother with two children, four and six years old. A social worker by training, Tina works full-time and sends her children to day care and after-school care programs. Luckily, the programs are good ones and Tina feels her children are happy and well adjusted. She wishes she could say the same about herself. Never married, Tina became pregnant with her first child "by accident." Since she was not in a relationship with the child's father, Tina chose to raise her son alone. With the support of friends and family, Tina made it through the first couple of years pretty well. Then she became involved with a man she really cared for. They had been living together for six months when she became pregnant with her second child. Shortly after that, Tina's boyfriend became panicked about the prospects of being in a committed relationship and having to support a young family. He loved her, he told Tina, but he just wasn't ready for all those responsibilities. That was the last she heard from him.

Four years later, Tina wasn't even angry at him anymore—she was glad, she told the group, that he left when he did rather than later. Why was she depressed? Like Charlene, she didn't know. It wasn't a fear of being alone, though, or because she didn't know how to please herself. She knew *how,* but she just didn't have the time or the money to do it. As Tina described her life of caring for the children, working, maintaining the household, everyone in the group felt exhausted just listening to her. No wonder she was depressed; Tina didn't have any time for her-

self. And she had two little children who were de-
lightful, but were also quite a handful for a single
parent. The therapy group was very sympathetic to
Tina and offered her a great deal of support and encouragement to help her to take care of herself. They
helped her to see that she would be a better mother
(her major concern) if she could make some time to
value her own needs as an individual.

Like Tina, mothers of young children are at higher
risk for depression. A study conducted in England
found that the presence of young children in the home
is a major factor contributing to depression among
women (regardless of marital status). The demands of
caring for young children, combined with the likelihood
that many mothers of young children are also employed
outside of the home, create a great deal of stress for
women in this situation. These factors do not affect fathers with young children in the same manner. Clearly,
the social roles for fathers and mothers, or for men and
women, are different.

Employment seems to have general beneficial effects
for women, as women who are employed are less depressed than women who are not employed, including
housewives. However, while employment is beneficial,
it doesn't protect women from depression as much as
it does men. In a study of women physicians, researchers found that the suicide rate for female doctors was
6.5 percent higher than that of male doctors and four
times higher than the suicide rate for white American
females of the same age as the women doctors.

While further studies need to be conducted to substantiate these findings, they do suggest that some professional women might be at greater risk for depression and suicide than other women or even their male counterparts in the same profession.

There have been a number of theories proposed as to why more women than men suffer from depression. It's unlikely that depression will ever be found to be due solely to one factor. Instead, there are a number of complex factors that might increase women's vulnerability to depression, including biological factors such as women's hormonal functioning, particularly during the postpartum period; socialization practices such as indoctrination of social roles and values of femininity; discrimination in employment and other aspects of society; risk factors for depression including dependence on interpersonal relationships, the demands of motherhood in raising small children, and even possible factors such as employment in nontraditional roles.

Whatever the cause, the fact remains that women are depressed in twice the numbers as men. This reality places women at particular risk for depression and it challenges mental health professionals to find ways to prevent, treat, and understand the unique aspects of depression in women. Since there is some evidence that women become depressed, at least in part, because of social discrimination factors and traditional sex-role stereotypes, treatment for women who are depressed should take these external factors into account. One successful treatment technique has been the short-term therapy group, led by an experienced psychotherapist. The advantage of a small therapy group (see chapter 6) is that it gives individual members the opportunity to share their personal experiences in the context of a discussion of situational risk factors, including interpersonal relationships, financial difficulties, the demands of raising children, employment issues, and the social status of women. In this chapter, many generalizations have been made as to how depression affects women as a group. When you consider your own risk factors or the risk factors of someone you know, it is best to view each individual depression as caused by a number of factors, and understand it through the consideration of a life history. Then the important task of designing a prevention and treatment plan can begin.

Depression in Children

Special Considerations
Matthew was only six years old when he was admitted to the psychiatric unit at Children's Hospital. The night before, his mother had brought him to the emergency room with minor burns on his arms. How did he get those burns? Matthew's mother, Sara, was visibly shaken and perplexed as she described how she woke up in the middle of the night on hearing Matthew's cries for help. She raced into the kitchen, where she found her son standing in front of their gas stove with his blanket. The blanket had just caught fire when Sara grabbed it from Matthew and smothered it, putting the fire out. Luckily, Matthew's burns were minor and he would recover quickly, reassured the emergency room doctor. But why was Matthew holding a blanket in front of a lit gas burner? At first, Matthew would not

speak to the doctor and just shook his head "no" to all questions. Frustrated, the doctor tried another strategy: she borrowed a play kitchen from the children's playroom and asked Matthew to tell a story of how a little boy woke up in the middle of the night and played with fire. Matthew liked the play kitchen with the shiny pots and pans. He started to play with the utensils. Eventually, he told the story of how a little boy felt so scared and alone that he wanted to get his mommy's attention by starting a big fire in the kitchen. Concerned that Matthew was very upset and at risk for harming himself or others, the doctor asked Sara to take Matthew to the children's psychiatric unit. She explained that Matthew's behavior was of major concern and that the clinicians on the unit would be able to evaluate the situation further.

Sara was very frightened by the entire episode and agreed, although she was reluctant to have contact with professionals. She was afraid they would blame her for not taking good enough care of her son.

As it turned out, the clinical team, made up of psychiatrists, psychologists, social workers, and nurses, spent the next couple of days playing and talking with both Matthew and his mother. They gathered a great deal of information, including a complete personal and family history for Matthew. When the case conference was held the next day, they invited Sara to attend so that she could understand what conclusions the team had come to, and what their recommendations were. Despite Matthew's young age, the clinicians felt that he was an unusually bright and sensitive child.

Two years earlier, his father had left the family after

a big fight with Sara. Matthew felt very sad about his father's absence, but was afraid to talk to his mother about it, because she would become upset and cry. Matthew wasn't sure why his father left and wondered if his father was angry at him. He felt sure that his father didn't care about him or his mother anymore, because he never called or visited. Sara was also very sad that her husband had left. She tried her best to appear cheerful and take care of Matthew, but she was quite depressed and overwhelmed at having to care for a child as well as work full time and pay the rent alone. So both she and Matthew muddled along for a while, neither of them doing very well. Then this year, Matthew started attending kindergarten. He had a hard time adjusting to the new school and made very few friends. Matthew admitted that he felt very alone, and when he tried to get his mother to pay more attention to him, sometimes it worked but other times she was too tired or depressed herself to meet his needs.

Matthew began to display symptoms of his own unique depression. He withdrew into his own fantasy world with make-believe friends and adventures. One of these adventures involved saving an entire house of people from a fire. In his fantasy, Matthew became a hero and everyone in his school knew who he was. His mother was very proud of him. Even his father read about him in the newspapers and came home because he was so proud of Matthew. So one night Matthew decided to start a fire, then rescue everyone. But it didn't work out the way he planned. He hadn't expected the flames to spread so quickly and he cried for help. Luckily, help came, in the form of his mother and the treatment team at the hospital.

Many children are not as fortunate as Matthew because their depression is not brought to the attention of helpers. Since the symptoms of depression are not necessarily the same for children as for adults, they are frequently missed by both families and professionals. Developmental factors must be considered in evaluating depression in children. For example, there are major differences in the development of intellectual, language, and social abilities according to the age of the children. Given these differences, it would make sense to assume that children's experiences and the way they express their depression will also vary according to their age. It is particularly difficult to assess depression in children because a number of problematic behaviors can be seen along with depression, including running away behavior, bed-wetting, loss of appetite, truancy, poor school performance, and aggressive behaviors. Since these behaviors are fairly common, it is not easy to determine if depression is present.

What Is the Prevalence of Childhood Depression?

Given the inconsistency of symptoms of childhood depression, it has been difficult to accurately measure how many children actually suffer from this illness. Some studies have suggested that about 5 to 10 percent of children are depressed, a slightly lower rate than in the adult population. Other studies have estimated that, among families with a history of depression, particularly in the parents, up to 30 to 50 percent of the children are depressed. Until diagnostic criteria of depression among children are more widely known and agreed upon, it may not be possible to find accurate numbers. Most researchers agree that, similar to the adult population, there are probably more depressed children than data would suggest.

Symptoms of Depression in Children: Developmental Aspects

Depressed children may or may not show the same symptoms as depressed adults. Sadness, for instance, is a part of depression for both children and adults, but children may not report feeling sad or even look sad. Instead, children sometimes express sadness by seeming bored, withdrawn, or even angry. Because children do not have the language abilities to describe or even to understand their emotions the way adults do, they tend to express their depression in their behavior. What form this behavior takes is dependent upon the age, and therefore, the developmental stage that the child is in. Some common expressions of depression for each developmental stage are:

Infant—"Failure to thrive" syndrome
   Little or no weight gain
   Lack of bonding with caretakers
   Little interest in new things

Toddler—"Terrible twos and more"
   Prolonged temper tantrums
   Sleep disturbances
   Refusal to eat
   Aggressive behavior

Preschool—"I don't have to"
   Oppositional behavior
   Aggressive behavior
   or
   Withdrawn behavior
   Difficulties with other children
   Sleeping and eating problems

Elementary school child—"School problems"
   Avoids school
   Poor school performance
   Physical ailments such as headaches and
      stomachaches
   Poor peer and adult relationships
   Daydreams all the time
   Aggressive physical behavior

Adolescent—"Leave me alone"
   Eating disorders (particularly in girls)
   Physical aggressiveness (particularly in boys)
   Extreme rebellious behavior
   Suicidal thinking
   Alcohol and drug use
   Antisocial behavior such as stealing, lying
   Some adultlike depression symptoms (such as
      sadness, feeling bad about oneself, and a loss of
      interest in previously enjoyable activities)

This is just a guideline to some of the common symptoms for each developmental level. Some symptoms of adult depression are probably applicable to older children, but usually children do not express more complex emotions, such as hopelessness and feelings of extreme guilt. Children are less able to internalize feelings and more likely to act out through aggressive behavior and physical complaints.

Frequently, it is not the parents who are first aware of the symptoms of depression, but the day-care providers or teachers who work with the child during the day. Parents are generally not aware that the behavior they see in their child is unusual, and report that their child "has always been a little different," or "I thought it was just a stage that she would outgrow." One thing that parents sometimes do notice is when the child's behavior suddenly changes, such as when active children suddenly seem to lose their energy or shy children become very aggressive. Teachers frequently notice that children will seem "out of it" because they are daydreaming a lot. Like Matthew, children will frequently live in their own fantasy world populated with pretend characters. When they carry the fantasy too far, it can become a problem and is generally indicative of problems with depression.

In many cases, depression develops after a loss of someone important to the child. A child can be devastated by the loss of parents, grandparents, siblings, good friends, neighbors, or even a beloved pet. In addition, separation or divorce of parents are two of the most stressful life events that children can experience. If children do not have the opportunity to express their feelings about such events in a constructive way, they will express them in other, less appropriate ways.

In general, depressed children feel isolated with their feelings. They believe that they have no one who can understand what they are experiencing, and usually don't trust anyone to accept them as they are. Their homes are not necessarily abusive or even neglectful, but their parents are frequently preoccupied, overworked, or depressed themselves, and unable to see the child's need for help. Sometimes parents of depressed children have overly high expectations of their offspring. The children have a strong desire to win their parents' approval but become depressed when they feel that they cannot possibly meet their expectations. Children can be particularly vulnerable because they are dependent on their parents for love and acceptance. If a child is emotionally neglected by his or her parents, he or she will try many things to win the parents' acceptance. Instead of acknowledging the parents' responsibility for the neglect, the child will consider himself or herself "bad." This is easier for children than understanding the failure of their parents to meet their needs, or realizing and looking forward to a time when things could change for the better. This self-blaming leads to the loss of self-esteem that is so common among both children and adults who are depressed.

It's extremely important for depressed children to get help. Sometimes parents and other adults think that children will "grow out" of their distress. This is rarely the case, if they don't receive professional help. If the warning signs of depression are ignored, it is more likely that the children will grow into unhappy adolescents, and the risk of suicide increases dramatically when children become adolescents. Reported suicides are the third most common cause of death among adolescents. The actual number of suicides is estimated to be much higher (as much as 50 percent higher) because so many "accidental deaths" may actually be suicides. And the risk of suicide among teenagers who feel isolated and different, such as lesbian and gay youth or pregnant teenagers, is no doubt even higher.

Treatment of Depression in Children and Adolescents

What kinds of treatment are most helpful for depressed children and adolescents? Pretty much the same kinds that are effective for adults: treatment programs that educate and involve the entire family, individual and group psychotherapy, and behavioral programs that work toward developing more rewarding behaviors. With children and teens, it is, of course, even more vital to include the entire family in the treatment because a young person's world is so controlled by the family interaction. Therapy groups are a place where children can share their problems with each other and feel less alone in their depression.

When looking for a clinician for your child or adolescent, you should seek a professional who specializes in working with children and teenagers. Frequently, school guidance counselors, pediatricians, or staff at children's hospitals can refer you to clinicians whose specialty is helping children. These child specialists may use play therapy as well as talking and listening to children to help them express their feelings and concerns. They will try to understand your child's or adolescent's unique problems and will usually work together with the family to develop a plan to help the child or teenager.

Adolescents sometimes need more autonomy and may prefer to work on their own with a clinician without help from the family. This autonomy should be encouraged, but parents should be kept informed about their child's progress without breaching confidentiality. Some teenagers may feel more comfortable participating in a group therapy session with other teens who are experiencing similar problems, while others prefer to talk to a therapist on a one-on-one basis. The type and style of therapy does depend upon your child or teen and what he or she prefers. Usually, even children or teenagers who are initially reluctant to see a therapist will be willing to work with someone once they discover that the clinician is there to help them understand their concerns and help them figure out ways to feel better.

It is much less common to use antidepressant medication with children and adolescents because there is more uncertainty about the effect of these medications on growing bodies. Since manic-depressive illness is rarely diagnosed in individuals younger than eighteen, the use of lithium is also limited.

The good news about depression among children and teens is that the course of a depressive episode is usually much shorter and the success rate in treating symptoms is much higher than in adults. Much as children recover more quickly from physical illness or surgery than adults do, their adaptability also enables them to get over their depression faster. When a depressed child or teenager receives the help he or she needs, the prognosis for a full recovery is very good, with little or no risk of recurrence.

Depression in the Elderly

Special Issues

Just as there are unique aspects and symptoms of depression among children, the same is true of the elderly. Studies have estimated the rate of depression among the elderly in the United States at 20 to 30 percent. Since the majority of the elderly are women, and women have a higher rate of depression overall, the rate of depression among the elderly is just slightly higher than among the general population.

Several social reasons have been proposed to explain the high risk of depression among the elderly. First, they commonly experience a number of life transitions in a short period of time: retirement and the accompanying reduction in income and daily routine; possible loss of spouses, friends, and family; possible loss of physical strength, independence, and mobility; increased vulnerability to crime; and having to cope with age discrimination.

There are also medical factors that place the elderly at higher risk for depression, since the elderly take more medications, including some (such as drugs to control high blood pressure and hormones such as prednisone) that may cause symptoms of depression. Common medical conditions, including hypothyroidism and Parkinson's disease, also produce symptoms of depression and are more prevalent in the elderly population.

Symptoms and Treatment

The symptoms of depression may be different for the elderly than for middle-aged adults. Instead of substantial changes in mood, depressed elderly tend to have more physical complaints such as general aches and constipation, and they become more isolated and withdrawn. Depression is likely to be underdiagnosed or misdiagnosed because physicians mistake physical symptoms for medical conditions, instead of seeing underlying depression. The psychological symptoms, such as being withdrawn or being disoriented, are frequently mistaken for senility or dementia. When older people become forgetful, move much more slowly, become more set in their ways, and become despondent about their situation, there is a tendency to attribute these characteristics to senility. Many people view senility as if it were an inevitable part of the aging process. In reality, many of these older individuals may be suffering from depression, a very treatable illness.

Lillian, seventy-five, could be considered typical of many elderly women. She was in reasonably good health but moved a bit slower than she did even five years ago. Widowed for four years, she still lived what she considered to be an independent life. Lillian maintained her own apartment and received just enough money from Social Security, pensions, and her two children to get by. A physically active person most of her life, Lillian felt frustrated by the arthritis that affected her fingers and legs. On good days she could still go on long walks, but on bad days she was barely able to get out of bed. Recently, Lillian was beginning to feel more discouraged about her decreased mobility and what she felt was her declining health. In addition, she realized that she was a vulnerable target for crime when she went out alone because she could not move very quickly if attacked. As a result, she became more dependent on her children to come and take her shopping on weekends. Lillian hated having to depend on other people, even on her children.

Like many elderly women, Lillian's feelings of vulnerability made her more fearful of going out and being active. The more she stayed in her apartment, the bleaker her life seemed and the more depressed she became.

Finally, she felt so unhappy with her life situation that she told her doctor she didn't have much to live for anymore. Acknowledging that Lillian had a right to feel depressed, her doctor then suggested that she first undergo a complete physical examination to rule out any medical conditions that might cause the depression. Then he started Lillian on a trial of antidepressant medication and recommended participation in a therapy group for older women. Figuring that she had nothing to lose, she agreed to try both approaches. Like most of the elderly, Lillian responded well to treatment and her group supported her in finding ways to become more active again. After two months, she still had her bad days, but in general she felt more optimistic about her ability to do things and to remain active.

As with younger adults, a combined treatment program of antidepressant medication and psychotherapy appears to be the most effective treatment for major depression in the elderly. The elderly are less likely to suffer from manic-depression unless they have a previous history of manic-depressive illness. In the few cases of manic-depression, lithium is still considered to be the most effective treatment, with extra precautions taken to control the level of lithium in the blood, since older people metabolize lithium more slowly than do younger individuals.

In spite of the many vulnerabilities to depression among the elderly, there is hope that the situation will improve as this population becomes greater in number. The medical profession is understanding the unique needs of elderly patients better than ever, and the elderly themselves are taking active roles in their own advocacy. There is every reason to believe that with increased knowledge of the special issues of aging and the aging process, as well as with new, more effective treatment programs, the incidence of depression among the elderly will soon decrease.

8

Looking to the Future: Resources to Help You

Not very long ago, depression was misunderstood, misdiagnosed, and mistakenly thought to be the result of a character defect or weakness. What treatment did exist usually focused on a long and often painful process geared toward understanding the lifelong "personality problems" of the individual. When that process was too time-consuming or a person was at too high a risk for suicide, ECT (electroconvulsive therapy) would be administered as a last resort. Given the few treatment options available, it's no wonder that those who suffered from depression, as well as their families and friends, continued to feel hopeless about their chances for recovery.

In the past two decades, we have made major strides in understanding and treating depression. We now know that it is the most common psychiatric illness, with at least 20 percent of all Americans suffering from major depression at some point in their lives. We also know that depression is not a result of a character flaw, but that some people are born with a genetic predisposition to being depressed. As with many medical conditions, such as heart disease or diabetes, if members of your family have been depressed, you are at a much higher risk for depression yourself. The new understanding of the biological basis of depression has done much to remove its old stigma as a shameful mental illness.

Because of this new knowledge, we also know more about prevention and effective treatment. Scientists are working to put together the puzzle that will explain *how* depression is passed on in the genes. There is hope that in the near future scientists will be able to identify a gene marker that would enable them to determine whether an individual has inherited the "depression gene." This would be a remarkable breakthrough, enabling parents to identify whether their child is at risk for depression from an early age and allowing families to work closely with professionals in planning preventive treatment that might make the difference between productive lives and lives filled with misery and despair.

With hope, the day when families will have that information is not far off. But until then, it's best for people with a family history of depression to assume that every family member is at risk and to act accordingly. Reading this book is a start, but you must continue to inform other family members about their risk for this illness. Much *is* known about depression and how you can shape your environment to reduce risk factors.

The treatment methods are quite diverse. If one treatment doesn't seem to be effective, then try others. There's no longer any reason for anyone to suffer in silence—or to suffer at all. Almost anyone can make a complete recovery from depression when it's properly diagnosed and treated, especially when family and close friends are included in the process.

We also know that we can reduce environmental risk factors by controlling stress (through exercise, for example), developing meaningful interpersonal relationships, cultivating a positive mindset, and attending support and therapy sessions. In larger cities and towns, there are depression clinics that are geared toward providing services to manic-depressed and depressed people. They are frequently affiliated with teaching hospitals or medical schools and sometimes conduct research studies to evaluate the effectiveness of various treatment methods. Sometimes you can participate in a study and receive free treatment or even be paid a small amount for your participation. You can usually find out about these clinics by calling the psychiatry department in medical schools or hospitals.

Aside from teaching facilities, some places to look for referrals for professional help include your family doctor, friends, your minister, rabbi, or priest, and your community or county mental health center. Also, your state licensing board can tell you if an individual is licensed to practice in your state.

Professional Organizations and Clearinghouses

The following are some excellent sources for information. They may be able to find the right therapist for you or answer some questions you might have.

American Academy of Child and Adolescent Psychiatry
3615 Wisconsin Avenue N.W.
Washington, DC 20016
(202) 966-7300

American Association for Marriage and Family Therapy
1100 17th Street N.W.
10th Floor
Washington, DC 20036
(202) 452-0109

American Psychiatric Association
Division of Public Affairs
1400 K Street N.W.
Suite 250
Washington, DC 20005
(202) 682-6220

Canadian Mental Health Association
National Office
2160 Yonge Street
Toronto, Ontario
M4S 2Z3
Canada
(416) 484-7750

Depressive and Manic Depressive Association of Ontario
214 Merton Street
Suite 101
Toronto, Ontario
M4S 1A6
Canada
(416) 481-5413

Foundation Quebecoise de Maladies Mentals
212 St. Joseph Boulevard
Montreal, Quebec
H2T 2P8
Canada
(514) 270-5354

Ontario Psychological Association
730 Yonge Street #221
Toronto, Ontario
M4Y 2B7
Canada
(416) 961-5552

American Psychological Association
750 First Street, N.E.
Washington, DC 20002-4242
(202) 336-5500
(202) 336-6123 TDD

Association for Advancement
  of Mental Health
145 Witherspoon Street
Princeton, NJ 08542
(609) 924–7174

National Mental Health Association, Inc.
1021 Prince Street
Alexandria, VA 22314
(703) 684–7722

National Alliance for the
  Mentally Ill
2101 Wilson Boulevard
Suite 302
Arlington, VA 22201
(703) 524–7600

National Association for Ru-
  ral Mental Health
12300 Twinbrook Parkway
Suite 320
Rockville, MD 20852
(301) 984–6200

National Association of Social
  Workers (NASW)
7981 Eastern Avenue
Silver Spring, MD 20910
(301) 565–0333

National Council of Community Mental Health Centers
12300 Twinbrook Parkway
Suite 320
Rockville, MD 20852
(301) 984–6200

National Depressive and
  Manic Depressive
  Association
730 North Franklin
Suite 501
Chicago, IL 60610
(312) 642–0049

For Further Reading

You can continue to inform yourself and others by
reading more about depression and manic-depression.
A few books that are suggested include:

David D. Burns, M.D. *Feeling Good: The New Mood Therapy.*
    New York: William Morrow, 1980.
Mark Gold with Lois B. Morris. *The Good News About De-
    pression: Cures and Treatments in the New Age of Psychi-
    atry.* New York: Bantam Books, 1986.

John H. Greist and James W. Jefferson. *Depression and Its Treatment: Help for the Nation's #1 Mental Problem*. Washington, D.C.: American Psychiatric Press, 1984.

Kathleen McCoy. *Coping with Teenage Depression: A Parent's Guide*. New York: New American Library, 1982.

Demitri Papolos and Janice Papolos. *Overcoming Depression*. New York: Harper & Row, 1987.

Pamphlets include:

"Depressive Illnesses: Treatments Bring New Hope." Marilyn Sargent, U.S. Department of Health and Human Services. National Institute of Mental Health (NIMH), 1989.

Write to:
National Institute of Mental Health (NIMH)
Information Resources and Inquiries Branch
5600 Fishers Lane
Rockville, MD 20857

The advances we have made in understanding the genetic aspects of depression hold great promise for the future—for ourselves, for our children, and for future generations.

Depression was once thought of as a tragedy that ruined people's lives and left them weak; now we have come to understand that people who suffer from depression are anything but weak. To survive in the midst of such despair and pain requires great courage and perseverance.

Glossary

Affective disorders. Mood disorders in which severe and inappropriate emotional responses and disturbances of mood occur, such as in depression and bipolar disorder.

Bipolar disorder. An affective disorder in which episodes of mania alternate with episodes of depression. Also known as manic-depression.

Confidant. A trusted friend with whom feelings, concerns, and personal difficulties can be shared. Having a confidant seems to guard against depression in some cases.

Gene. The unit of genetic material and inheritance.

Genetics. The branch of biology concerned with the principles and mechanics of heredity.

Heredity. The process by which traits and characteristics are transmitted from parents to offspring.

Major endogenous depression. An affective disorder characterized by symptoms such as insomnia, lethargy, psychomotor retardation, and a dysphoric, hopeless mood. Unlike exogenous depression, the factors that lead to endogenous depression are not identifiable and its causes are complex, probably involving biochemical, psychological, interpersonal, and sociocultural factors.

Major exogenous depression. A depressive disorder caused by a reaction to an identifiable external situation or event, such as a divorce or the death of a loved one, or an internal emotional conflict. Also sometimes called reactive depression or situational depression.

Maladaptive. Defective adaptation to stress or change.

Mania. The phase of bipolar disorder characterized by agitation, overexcitement, increased psychomotor activity, and sometimes violent and self-destructive behavior.

Monoamine oxidase (MAO) inhibitors. A class of drug used to treat depression.

Psychiatry. The branch of medical science concerned with mental, emotional, and behavioral disorders.

Psychomotor. Relating to voluntary muscular movement associated with conscious mental activity. In a depressive episode, psychomotor activity is slowed; during the manic phase of bipolar disorder it is accelerated.

Psychotherapy. The treatment of mental and emotional disorders through verbal communication (rather than medical treatments) with a qualified therapist.

Tricyclic. A class of antidepressant drug used to treat endogenous depression.

Unipolar depression. A mood disorder involving depressive symptoms only.

Index